I
HAD
A
FATHER

OTHER BOOKS BY CLARK BLAISE

I
HAD
A
FATHER

A POST-MODERN
AUTOBIOGRAPHY

CLARK BLAISE

ADDISON-WESLEY PUBLISHING COMPANY

READING, MASSACHUSETTS   MENLO PARK, CALIFORNIA
NEW YORK   DON MILLS, ONTARIO   WOKINGHAM, ENGLAND
AMSTERDAM   BONN   SYDNEY   SINGAPORE   TOKYO   MADRID
SAN JUAN   PARIS   SEOUL   MILAN   MEXICO CITY   TAIPEI

Portions of this book have appeared previously in a somewhat different form in the *New York Times Magazine* ("His" column); *Iowa Review; Salmagundi;* Borderlands Monograph Series (Canadian-American Center, U. of Maine); Contemporary Authors Autobiography Series (Gale Research Co., Detroit). An earlier autobiographical-fictional volume, *Resident Alien* (Penguin Canada) contains the seeds of a few events expanded upon here.

The excerpt from Frederick Feirstein's poem, "The Film Maker to His Father," has been reprinted with permission from *Survivors* (David Lewis, New York, 1974).

Many of the designations used by manufacturers and sellers to distinguish their products are claimed as trademarks. Where those designations appear in this book and Addison-Wesley was aware of a trademark claim, the designations have been printed in initial capital letters (i.e., Formica).

Library of Congress Cataloging-in-Publication Data

Blaise, Clark.
   I had a father : a post-modern autobiography / Clark Blaise.
     p. cm.
   ISBN 0–201–58128–0
   1. Blaise, Clark—Biography—Family. 2. Novelists, Canadian—20th
century—Biography. 3. Fathers and sons—Canada—Biography.
I. Title.
PR9199.3.B48Z465   1993
813′.54—dc20
[B]
                                            92–29079
                                                CIP

Jacket design by Virginia Evans
Text design by Barbara Cohen Aronica
Set in 11-point Bembo by Westchester Book Composition

1 2 3 4 5 6 7 8 9-MU-9796959493
First printing, February 1993

To Bart and Bernard,
who have one

CONTENTS

I had an ethnic father, but not an ethnic childhood. In recent years, however, I've grown increasingly fascinated with a life not quite my own that might have been mine *si j'avais choisi le chemin de mon père.* That is, if I had followed my father's course as a French-Canadian (born Léo Roméo Blais in 1905, in Lac-Mégantic, Québec) or as a Franco-American (died Lee R. Blaise in 1978, in Manchester, New Hampshire). The fascination with my father, which is really an exploration of my own sense of incompleteness, found some expression in two recent story collections (*Resident Alien* and *Man and His World*), but they were fictions pushing forward to resolution instead of backward to the mystery of origins. The years are whizzing by now like kilometers instead of miles, and my imagination and memory are running together, as though watching myself and my prior selves being born.

Early in this century planetary mathematicians noted a slight perturbation in the orbit of the planet Neptune. That bump pointed to the existence of a dark planet beyond Neptune whose size and position could be confidently plotted. Astronomers knew where to look—that is, the geography was predictable—and what they were looking for. Only the magnifying and light-gathering tools were missing. That celebrated event might help explain my feelings toward my father, and the method of this book.

Sometimes you fool yourself, you think that once you've established the existence of a remote object, you don't have to pursue it. Now I would say: Follow your perturbations. Vacant space and occult gravities are the stuff of fiction. Lest I be accused of comparing the magnitude of my identity problems to the mass of a planet, I should say only that knowing *where* to look—the geography of ontogeny—does have a correlation to writing. Geography is destiny. Fiction and autobiography, like science, are based on observable responses to unknown forces. In fiction, the forces will be discovered and confronted. In autobiography the forces will be confronted and surmounted.

Looking on the face of my father long before I was born—seeing the parish entry of his birth, his employment files, his divorce papers, his police records, his death certificate—is, in an infinitesimal way, what astronomers must have felt when training their mechanical eyes on a quadrant of space and watching for telltale smears on their time-lapse plates and being able finally to say: Here it is, the last wanderer of our solar system. Call it Pluto. The planetary cast of characters is complete, let the play begin.

I have subtitled this book "a post-modern autobiography" to emphasize one point and to warn against a second. It is an attempt to fashion continuity from fragments and certainty from rumor. It is not a "life"—either mine (such as a public person might set down with the help of a ghost), or my father's. I have all the ghosting I need. Even now, I don't know if my father was sane or disturbed, a victim or a killer. I don't even know if I am his only child. I don't know, finally, if any of it matters. I have tried to deal with my ignorance openly; this is the autobiography of a consciousness fighting to achieve sovereignty over its own experiences.

I
HAD
A
FATHER

"...he would never be with her more than at the present moment. The surprise to come was that he wouldn't be with her less."

—Alice Munro, *Half a Grapefruit*

"Your nearest exit may be behind you."

—Standard airline evacuation instruction

I

MY LIFE

AS

AN ATLAS

I WAS THIRTY-EIGHT YEARS OLD when my father died, but I don't feel I had thirty-eight years of fathering. In fact, I've heard more from him in the dozen years since his death than I ever did when he was alive.

He reentered my life in 1984, six years after his death, because of the smell of cigarettes. He was a lifetime three-pack-a-day smoker, and his smoker's musk lingered in every room and attached itself to everything he touched. I was living in a furnished apartment in Atlanta, a writer-in-residence at Emory University, and the person who had preceded me in that apartment had left his traces in the air, on the walls, and in cigarette burns on the porcelain rims of the lavatory—the toilet tank lid and the bathtub. It was as though my father was trying to reach me. I suddenly remembered the thin coat of talcum powder he left on the floor, the *Readers' Digest* whose pages would wrinkle and stick in the condensation water next to the yellow box of Serutan on the lid of the tank. I remembered how he prepared the regal acts of shaving in the morning or of settling back in the tub with a tumbler of Scotch and a cigarette, pinching it so it wouldn't roll into the water. He would linger in the tub till the Scotch was finished and his wet fingers had dissolved the Herbert Taryton. The residue of tobacco strands, pubic hair, and talcum powder would be left for the next bather to clean up. The wreckage of the bathroom was a kind of male statement—the lion at ease—but also a sign of his retreat from us. In the period of my growing-up, my father communicated more through his leavings than his presence. He left an eloquent trail.

In that Atlanta apartment, the edges of the Formica dining table and the kitchen counters were nicked with little brown parabolas where a butt had smoldered to its filter. Where bad habits had left a scar.

The tribe of men and women who had preceded me had left a kind of archaeological record, a small-scale human history. Heedless, hard-smoking people will be gone in a decade. It's hard to see them now as *film noir* heroes or existential Bogarts or Belmondos after the U.S. Surgeon General has put them on notice. But they do embody the low-rent heroism of people, like my father, who ignore their weaknesses and the price they're going to pay. Foolish mortals with stories to tell.

In his last year, 1978, he was in a New Hampshire hospital where I came down to visit him every weekend from Montréal. He'd left Canada forty years earlier—I was the one who'd tried to reverse history by going back, becoming Canadian, and becoming French (the foolish mortal gene is dominant and comes from the father's side). He'd tried Florida and Pittsburgh, four marriages and dozens of liaisons, only to end his days in the traditional capital of Franco-America—Manchester, New Hampshire.

If anyone had told my father in his pioneering days in Florida or his glory years in Pittsburgh that he'd die and be buried in Manchester, his first American home, he might have killed himself on the spot.

(Several years after his death, I drove down to Manchester from his birthplace in Québec. I was checking out some of his old addresses, and I was confused between similar-sounding streets on the Yankee and French sides of the Merrimack. I asked a young woman who was digging a *Union-Leader* out of her newspaper tube where Boutwell Street was, and she thought hard before answering, "That's ovah in the Frag pand.") So my father was Frog Pond French from Manchester—born French in Canada, died English in Manchester—despite all his struggles and his lies to deny it.

He might never have known who or what he was, but anyone reading his obituary in the *Union-Leader* knew immediately: he was typical, with a typical birthplace, and a typical name, and a typical story to tell. In Manchester, when an old French-Canadian dies (three died in Manchester the same day he did), the obituary etiquette dictates only "born in Canada," which means French and Catholic, with mass and visitation and burial at the usual locations. In Manchester, *Canada* means only Québec.

I am attracted to that typicalness. And I am writing this book to deny it absolutely.

In his last years, the veins in his legs had collapsed, his feet were icy, and he was told he would never walk again. The surgical decision had been over the practical solution—amputation—or the riskier and far more expensive alternative of vascular transplants. The high-tech procedure won out. It was, perhaps, my father's final con job, convincing a gifted young surgeon that a $100,000 vascular rehab on a 70-year-old man without insurance was both cost-effective and repayable. It moves me—

knowing his Old World attitude to hospitals, that if you're sick enough to enter they won't let you out till they've cut something off or taken something out—his confidence that he'd be able to walk again, divorce again, and start a new little furniture store as soon as he could take possession of his full, forty-five years of Social Security. In his last months my father finally did walk on warm feet and died without touching a penny of his Social Security and owing the full amount on his operation.

But in those weeks just after the surgery, I held his feet in my hands, and they never warmed. He was turning into a corpse even as we spoke. I had him where I wanted him. Now we could talk. Now he could hold my books, perhaps even try to read them, and he would tell me, finally, about his life, the epic novel that he'd lived.

That's how it's supposed to work out. The genius of the male life span, the myth of fathers dying just as sons are ready to take their place. What a ragged little convention it is! I don't know any man my age who wouldn't want his father back, no matter how deformed their relationship had been. I don't know any man my age, with the possible exception of Philip Roth, who achieved a proper parting with his father, who didn't feel cheated of one last sailing, one last drink, one last drive to the sunset.

In our case, it didn't happen for another dozen years.

"Tell me, Dad," I might have said, jauntily. "You weren't always faithful to Mom, were you?"

"Well," he might have answered, "what man is? What man can be?" Another sip. "Are you?" I might dodge behind Donald Barthelme: "The beauty of women makes of adultery a serious moral decision." Behavior I could not

forgive in him twenty years ago, I take a different view
of now.

His is the voice that speaks to me whenever I write.
The best book that I can ever write would be his story,
and in those final months I wanted him to start telling it.
About Frenchness and hunger and death. The missing links
in that traditional Québec-to-Manchester immigrant pipe-
line. (When he married for the final time in 1963 to a
woman from Manchester, she took me aside and said,
"Your dad was quite a guy wasn't he? I've got a relative
in the police department who looked him up and told me
he's got a record as long as your arm." In her accent it
came out, *lang's yam*.)

I wanted to know about being the second-youngest
of eighteen, about having five siblings die in a single week,
about the medieval Catholicism of old Québec. About his
rum-running days during Prohibition, the shootouts, his
boxing (Kid Leo, the Fighting French Bantamweight),
his four marriages. Yes, and the police record. Such a simple thing to wonder about, and how it would have changed
my life had I known—do I have a brother or sister? What
made Léo Blais run, what made him into Lee Blaise?

HIS BACKGROUND HAD MADE HIM first a boxer, second
a salesman. He was a Golden Gloves champion, fighting
as Kid Leo, a bantamweight. He always told us he'd quit
after his first knockout, at the hands of "Battling Batta-
lino," an eventual professional champion. A seventeen-
and-a-half-inch neck on a bantamweight. A thin, raw line
around his neck every night from those starched white

shirts, like a tiny noose. My mother blamed boxing for everything in his life, from the "blackout" in Georgia that nearly killed him, to his moods and temper, his lies and his reckless behavior.

It's true that he was a trained boxer; when I was six or seven, I could stand in front of him trying to punch his face, big as a punching bag just inches away, with him weaving away from me on his knees, and I could never reach him. My father envelopes me like a language I don't remember learning, never use, but somehow remember. I remember my hands sweating inside those gloves and the sudden coolness when my mother, screaming, ripped them off.

For me, the business world was part of boxing. It was dog-eat-dog with the sleekest hounds rising to the top. I watched the process, the strategies, and the dirty tricks with evident panic. There was no place in it for me. I'd suffered through my childhood and adolescence, the insecurities of muscular betrayal, thyroid collapse, being a "husky" in the boy's section, shopping for disguise and not display, and the physical insecurities had formed my character. All I had going for me was a good mind and my mother's total support, both of which drove him even farther from me.

The addition of that single letter *e* to his name threw me out of orbit. There are dozens of pages of "Blais" in the Montréal phonebook. And at the end of them, in the fifteen years of our Montréal residence, there were three "Blaise's": a Clark, a Max, and a Rudi. By adding one lousy little letter, my father had condemned me to the alphabetical community of German-speaking Swiss Protestants. I still get genealogical inquiries from the Luxembourg Blaise Society. It's like Germanizing a Goldman by adding an *n*.

He'd had a marriage before my mother, though I never learned of it or even suspected its existence until my mother told me after their divorce. I took the revelation calmly, folded the name and date and place of marriage on a slip of paper (Delia Chartrand, 1925, Wethersfield, Connecticut), and tucked it in my wallet, where it stayed for years. Twelve years, 1925–1937, a substantial marriage, third-longest of his marrying career.

That first marriage was the great secret in my growing-up years, I realize now, though I can't imagine why it was so shameful. The unspeakable divorce was a Pluto-like invisibility that enforced a kind of innocence on him — that he'd had no life before I was born. He'd just been a hard-working bachelor too poor to marry whom my crafty mother had lured into marriage. He was cute and shy and ambitious; she'd broken through his reserve, seen the diamond underneath, and polished it. The artificial innocence had a second effect: sex was something unmentionable, sex was my mother's only realm of shame and secrecy. And keeping the secret of the marriage and divorce from me bought a kind of protection for her, and for me: *I won't tell the boy about Delia, but you must promise never to strike him, or me.*

I think now, holding a copy of that original 1937 Manchester divorce decree, issued just weeks before he married my mother in Montréal (my father was married for fifty-three years, to four women, and was never unmarried for longer than three weeks), the ultimate reason for keeping it secret was to protect himself from me. If I had known of his earlier life, I would have pestered him for facts. Sooner or later the fictions he maintained would have unraveled. His first married life carried him from age twenty to age thirty-two, the dark ages of his life. A baby boy was born, but died. In the past few years, the State of New Hampshire has destroyed all its police files of those years, the only record that would help me fill them in.

I would have asked, did you have children? Why did you leave her? Can I call her up?

The official reason for divorce: fear of mortal injury.

The father I remember was in his fifties, white and gray at the temples like a Latin lover, with dark glossy hair slicked down and parted in the middle. "Actually, Lee has wavy hair," my mother used to say to friends, "I wish he wouldn't plaster it down." (It is wavy in their honeymoon pictures and parted from the side their first summer in Montréal.) But after washing, when it was wavy, it was totally gray. I used to comb it for him when he sat in his chair in front of the television in Pittsburgh, combing it forward over his eyes, and the undergrowth was entirely white, like the underside of a fur-bearing mammal. Only when I combed it back did the white hairs nestle under the black.

I was my mother's son, never his—intellectually, morally, physically—so why, in middle age, should I feel only his encoding? The face I sense looking out on the world is his. At fifty, and depending on the season and the time available for outdoor running, I'm in better shape than I have ever been. I wouldn't shame him. We're a credible father and son now.

I REMEMBER A DAY in 1947, under the arcade of Main Street in the small, central Florida town of Leesburg. I was seven. We'd just come out of the bank with its dark, air-cooled lobby and its jug of free orange juice and tube of salt tablets, and I must have asked him for Coca-Cola money. He dug deep into the pocket of his high-waisted pants and came out with a handful of change. "That's it, son, that's all we've got." I understand now, he'd just been turned down for a bank loan. But at the time it thrilled me; in the movies, deliverance arrived at the darkest hour and I believed profoundly in Hollywood plotting. I was sacrificing a Coke to a good cause.

My childhood was like the weather; be patient and we might be back in Canada or a place with snow, a place with streetcars, or mountains. If he had been able to buy any of the properties we rented or to hold on to any of the businesses he started, the rising property values would have made him rich. Our Florida years were spent visiting resettled Yankees, World War II veterans younger than my father who'd established themselves in air-conditioned mansions on beaches or lakefronts, with ocean-going yachts and Bahamian servants, living like colonial barons in some unthreatening Third World sweatbox. Which, of course, Florida was. We never rose above the rented sweat-boxes, or worse.

When he was fifty, in 1955, he began the lone suc-cessful operation of his life. We worked through a Pitts-burgh summer converting a landmark suburban restaurant into a furniture store, boarding up the fake-Viking fire-place, and sealing the cracks in the meat locker with gallons of embalming fluid. We presented the bank with a *fait accompli,* sweat of our brows, and they gave him a loan to stock the store. ("Only because of you, Mrs. Blaise," the loan-officer told my mother. "Your husband, frankly, scares me.") And the amazing thing for a family that had known only insecurity and failure was that for six years it, and a second store, prospered. The store got me through three years of college. It bought the only house we ever owned. He would have been a rich man if he'd been able to hold on to it. Then a new woman entered his life and he lost everything.

Besides his cigarettes I remember now the lingering smell of stale meat and the acrid, caked soot from the fireplace. That it should come down to this—a father, odors only! He died with his stories intact, and if I am to bring him back I must reconstruct him from smoke. As I enter my fifties, I find that I have absorbed him, we are becoming one. His world is gone, or going fast. Middle age is the final orphanage.

WITHOUT BEING RELIGIOUS, I believe in a universe of fixed forms, in a moral shape to our lives, even in a kind of all-enveloping plot. Repeated actions lead to predictable consequences. One subplot is the grown man's search for his dead father, for understanding a connection between them that was denied in life. Making moral sense out of mortal fragments. His example, his life and death, must mean something to me; he's the only man with my genes who's been my age. He imprinted me.

There are no shortcuts in this search, no Deep Throats to step out of the mists and take me aside. No rabbit holes to tumble down, like Alice, into a distorted version of everyday reality. (*Alice in Wonderland,* for me, is the great modernist novel.) Or else the Deep Throats and rabbit holes are all around me, in these scarred tabletops and tobacco odors—the moral universe trembles with immanence. In defiance of classic logic, two entities can co-exist in the same time and place, but only in different dimensions. Those dimensions are memory and imagination.

CHAPTER TWO

I AM WRITING THESE SENTENCES on a laptop computer on an *estancia* in north-central Argentina, with a blown-over, shallow-rooted eucalyptus, long and silvery and misplaced as a yacht in the middle of an English garden, just in front of my line of vision. A new trail bike is propped against a peeling, metal column. Aspiration and limitation, I think; scale and vulnerability. The moral universe still speaks.

A week ago I was in New Zealand, earnestly discussing everyone's Commonwealth identity crises. Three days later in my graduate seminar in Iowa City (Exogenous Literatures: the English novel from non-American, non-British sources), I was teaching Thomas Keneally's *Schindler's List,* a documentary novel by an Australian about Oskar Schindler, a "good German," and his protection of Jews in his Cracow enamel factory during World War II. And the next morning, I left for Argentina.

The world, in other words, has opened up for me. Three continents in a week is extreme but not uncommon. Travel itself means less than it ever has, which doesn't alter the fact that travel has become my life. Travel has always been my life, first from the pages of an atlas, then from the back of a car. It is by now something other than arrival and departure; it is a form of obliteration and renewal. I'm a professional traveler. I travel the world for literature.

My father was a traveling salesman. Between 1938 and 1945, he worked for Sears, ending in Pittsburgh, then he pocketed his benefits and launched himself in Atlanta. "The road" was for him, as it is for me, a life of constant self-invention. He "covered Dixie," according to his letterhead, though in fact he did little more than crisscross southern Georgia and northern Florida in the late '40s. He didn't even have Jacksonville.

ACCORDING TO THE AUTHOR'S INTRODUCTION, *Schindler's List* began writing itself from the moment Keneally entered a leather-goods store in Beverly Hills and bought a briefcase. The owner of the store was a Holocaust survivor and a "Schindler Jew," named Leopold Pfefferberg. One does not expect the moral universe to rent an address in Beverly Hills. It was not a leather-goods shop; it was a rabbit hole. The great writers fall through it every time: Chekhov, Malamud, Babel, Keneally, Flannery O'Connor—they stand so firmly in moral traditions that the world speaks to them dramatically in moral terms.

If a tree falls in the forest and no one hears it, did the tree make a noise? Did a tree fall, or was it always fallen? Was Keneally waiting for Pfefferberg, or Pfefferberg for Keneally? Or was the story waiting for both of them? If I had a father and I knew nothing about him, saw no pictures of him, knew nothing of his life before my living memory, could I say I had a father? If I want to know him, I have to retrieve every scrap, inhale every whiff, subpoena every document related to him, pester the town clerks, hire a private investigator. Then I can invent him.

Family is all we know of infinity, the insolence of fate. We are born to strangers we must learn to love, in a town or country we would not have chosen, into a tribe that defines and restricts our growth. We spend a lifetime overcoming the givens, only to turn from the distant vantage point of fifty years when the parents are gone, to look back and say: this is what I am, something no larger, no freer, than they made me. I have seen the world, traveled to all its continents, have married far outside my tribes, have changed countries, citizenships, and have fathered sons who, if they think of such things at all, must wonder too at the infinity and insolence of their fates.

And I come back, like many an aging embryo (the phrase is Edwin Honig's), to the realization that I have aged into my father's likeness, into his patterns, and the years I spent fleeing him and his world have imprinted themselves deeply on me. I walk around, a late-developing negative, becoming his image after a lifetime of denial, of defining myself against his example.

Age and disappointment—the early and mid-'80s were not particularly kind to me—have caused me to reinvent my father. I have repackaged him. I have become more like him because my life became more like his. I learned the compassion for him that I should have felt at his dying, in the endless self-pity I was feeling for myself.

I THINK MY PARENTS WERE HAPPY in 1947 in central Florida. They were two years into their new, post-Sears, post-northern life. Already an Atlanta showroom he'd opened with his Sears nest egg had failed. And so, like any good French-Canadian, he'd followed his instincts and gone further south. We tried West Palm Beach for three or four months, then went north to Leesburg, midway between the two sizable towns of the region, Ocala and Orlando.

He started out as a traveling salesman (a "manufacturer's representative" in today's language) for various lines of furniture. It was the beginning of the post-War boom. Year-round residents were coming to Florida. Motels were springing up, all of them requiring cheap interchangeable furniture. Selling on the road was my father's fallback position; he wanted to manufacture furniture, or to own a store, because temperamentally he could not work in close quarters with other people. He was a natural salesman, a bit of a bully and cheat, a charmer and hustler. The road—setting his own times and his routes, driving all night, shaving in a gas station, drinking coffee and smoking in a diner till nine o'clock when the furniture stores opened up—was preferable to punching a clock and fighting other clerks for commissions. Motels were preferable to home. Restaurant meals were better than my mother's fish, chicken, organ meats, and broccoli. The company of the road suited him, drinks with his fellow salesmen, and a new woman every night.

The post-War boom was a great time for salesmen. The longing for new cars, new appliances, new designs, had replaced the barracks-lust for Betty Grable and Rita Hayworth. Every table aspired to having a lazy Susan, every bed an electric blanket, every kitchen a portable radio. When my father was home, we'd get him to drive to Daytona Beach, about forty miles away. On those uncluttered miles of white, powdered sand, I sat on his lap and steered. In a car, singing along with Bing Crosby—"Peg o' My Heart," "I'm Looking over a Four-Leaf Clover"—with a cigarette burning and his arm out the window and a woman—even his wife—beside him, he was happy.

We drove Chevies; a chrome strip splitting the windshield, which we'd have to scrape for bugs on those hot summer nights under a radiant moon. Chrome bars curved like fancy grillwork over the center of the dash. When he drove he didn't have to talk. He was making good time, as salesmen say, and making good money. He bought the first Chrysler Town & Country convertible in central Florida—a masterpiece of wood, chrome, and leather. He memorized maps, the same way I did. Like a local bus station announcer, he could rattle off the town names in order between any two cities on any southern highway. He knew the secret things that weren't on the maps but were vital in the South—speed traps, speakeasies in the dry counties, one-armed bandits in the back of certain gas stations. My world lay folded on my lap in two dimensions. His was the road and the life on the shoulders, unrolling under the hood ornament, in three dimensions.

These were his approachable moments, when he'd stop for soft ice cream without my begging. He was a talented crooner, he could have, *should have,* been an entertainer, he had all the pathologies of a public charmer, including a private repertoire of zero affect. He was the man who swept women off their feet, the gay blade, the Frenchman, whom women whispered about. I heard it all, but the family innocence protected me. I didn't know what they were talking about. I didn't know that compliments implied consequences. No one connected me, fat and blond, with him.

These are the elements of our life: radio, car, movement. Under its roof, my world is intact. All things are possible. And the tensions, unknown to me, are pulling me apart.

"Let's play the name game, Daddy," I suggest. My mother groans, "Dear, haven't you . . . "

"I've got a new one. I'll start." No complaint from my father yet. "Anderson."

"Aucoin."

"That's an O, Daddy. I win!"

"It's an A."

"Blaise," I say.

"Beaudoin."

"Chapman."

"Carrier."

I knew my strong letters—E, K, W—and I knew the treacherous pools of names at his command, the inexhaustible resources of names starting with B, and then the forest of L-names—"c'mon, Daddy, you can't just put a 'La' in front of words," I'd complain, with his Laplace and Laplante and La This and La That, but I'd yield to my mother's refereeing. "He's right, dear, we knew a janitor with that name . . . " or a politician or someone else they'd known back in Montréal. We'd lock ourselves in this strange combat off and on for hours. I kept an alphabetical list of classmates, teachers, actors, and radio-names, each new name with a new first letter was like a baseball card filling in the gaps. (God! To have some of those baseball cards today.) For some self-imposed reason he confined himself to the French names he'd grown up among, and when he didn't, when he borrowed from American names, I'd howl.

A few years later when we took longer drives to North Carolina for the furniture convention in High Point, I'd pick out the neon signs in the small towns. "Fortin!" I'd say, or "Ducharme," and the signs leaped out of an almost fictional world. They looked somehow right to me. I always looked for the nameplate of bus drivers, the proprietor's name over the front door of gas stations, places I associated with a high percentage of the names that populated our late-night drives.

WHEN IT ALL ENDED for him, after a "blackout" in south Georgia in a sidewalk-clearing accident at five in the morning that destroyed a blockful of parked cars and left our Chrysler Town & Country convertible just a folded can of wood and metal and my father with a broken back, shoulder, arms, and legs, and purple scars on the side of his head that never went away, there was a lady sitting with him in the hospital. When my mother got on the first Greyhound to Valdosta to see him after surgery, she was turned away, orders of the woman inside, "Mrs. Blaise."

He couldn't walk for six months, in a full body-cast, and we moved to a shanty in the woods without electricity or running water. Gone were the fancy car and the dinners out, the nightly Scotches. He rolled his own cigarettes, and I caught fish to support us. For a year we lived in the underbelly of the old South, among moss-pickers, migratory laborers too poor and disorganized even to aspire to sharecropping.

THIS IS THE OBSERVABLE EXTENT of my ethnic childhood. A game of names, a tribal extender. That, and listening to my father as he counted, or added figures, the numbers sinking into my brain as grunts and hisses, unh, duh, twa, cat, sank, sis, set, wit, nuff, dis.

When our younger son, Bernard, moved back to Montréal, city of his birth, in 1991, after a dozen years and a college degree in the United States, the bank computer scanned the name on his application for checks and automatically corrected the spelling. Montréal welcomed him as if it had known all along he, Bernard Blais, would come back and had kept his true identity waiting.

ON TOP OF ONE OF THE HIGHEST MOUNTAINS in
southeastern Québec stands a modern observatory. At
thirty-six hundred feet, the trip to the top of Mont-
Mégantic is more an outing than an adventure. Looking
over the haze-cast valleys at other blue ridges forty miles
away, it's easy to think you've reached one of the peaceful
spots on the eastern seaboard. The only sounds come from
chipmunks, birds, and the crunch of gravel in the parking
lot. The selection of Mont-Mégantic as a site is a monument to the vivid smear the Milky Way still leaves across
the nighttime sky. You realize suddenly that, like 90 percent of Americans, you have not seen the Milky Way,
really seen it, almost heard it crackle in its crispness, in
forty years.

The observatory is open to the public. A consortium
of astronomy departments at Laval University and the
University of Québec runs it. Graduate students give
guided tours. The corridors are lined with color photos,
like icons, of nebulae and novae, *nains blancs* and *géants
rouges* (white dwarfs and red giants).

All the visitors, this day at least, are French-speaking:
lean, moustached men in polyester pants, white shoes, and
white belts, their wives in floral dresses and stiff, blondish
wigs. I'm not a tall man, but I'm the tallest man here. The

men look familiar to me. I am probably related to someone here today, and Mégantic is the only place in the world where this might be true. Two hundred years of my father's family—hundreds of Blaises and their collateral relatives—have died within fifty miles of this mountain. My father and his seventeen brothers and sisters were all born ten miles away. My second and third cousins still live here. I am fifty, and this is my first visit.

These are small-town French-Canadians. They'd see themselves that way, as *canadiens, habitants,* not as upscaled, politicized *québécois.* They are quiet, Catholic, conventional people making peace with the slotted dome of advanced technology, nodding to their learned young tour-guides the way earlier generations might have surrendered authority under different domes to priests and politicians.

These mountain ridges are the northern spur of Appalachia. The language and the religion and even the look of the people have changed from the Carolinas and New England, but not the memories of hunting and fishing, the marginal life of quarrying and dairy farming, or even scrub-lumbering from the logged-out bush. And, of course, the insularity. The terrible, suffocating suspiciousness of outsiders, from Georgia to Cape Breton Island, the touchiness, the preference to be left alone.

WHEN MY WIFE AND I came back to the United States in 1980 and lived in Saratoga Springs, New York, we'd receive furtive knocks on the back door. There'd be a battered pickup truck in our driveway, its bed stacked with cordwood. "Saw your chimney. Need h'any wood?" the man would ask. Hewers of wood, drawers of water. Bad teeth, under-dressed for the cold, kids and a woman in the cab, and a handpainted name and phone number on the door. J–P Comtois. One of our French-Canadian names.

THE NORTH AMERICAN EXPERIMENT comes down to this: invading cultures preserving their heresies—English Puritanism and French Jansenism—and living in their shadows long after their disappearance in the mother countries. All that is slowly passing, but not the way we might have chosen. Signposts now dot the Québec roadsides: *Nos arbres ne peuvent combattre la pluie acide* (Our trees cannot stand up to acid rain). The old ways are shriveling, rather than fading away.

At the base of Mont-Mégantic lies the ambitiously named village of Piopolis, just a crossroads with a statue of a *zouave* in the middle. Population is now a couple of hundred, and dwindling. Piopolis means the "City of Pius," founded in the 1870s and named for the last fierce Pope, Pius IX, who spat out his vicar's curse of Infallibility and the Immaculate Conception on the modern world, and raised the army of mercenary zouaves to guard the Vatican against the popular cause of Garibaldi and Italian unification.

Poetic nationalism came to Québec a hundred years later.

An archaeologist, studying the zouave, might say *mark this statue: here the Middle Ages came to an end.* Piopolis is the last outpost of what Julia Kristeva has called the cult of God. Here the voyage of Catholicism into the New

World in its French and not its Spanish form left its final monument. My grandparents married about fifteen miles from Piopolis in 1882.

YOU MIGHT SAY my grandparents had a very long marriage. A three-hundred-year marriage with at least three thousand children. In 1892 one of my aunts, named Marie-Blanche, had five births and four deaths in a single year. Put that in a novel and I'd be accused of plagiarizing from Gabriel García Márquez.

YOU MUST ADJUST your sights and think of Canada, especially French Canada, as something mysterious, even magnificent, the way Bruce Beresford and Brian Moore did in their film *Black Robe*. (*Why is it only Australian filmmakers have the epic vision?*) In other words, you have to endow the experience with moral weight, however misguided. Otherwise, why should anyone care? In the great North American scheme of things, French-Canadians are under-achievers. I asked my father once who was the most famous French-Canadian? It took him a while to come up with Rudy Vallée. My mother countered with Gisèle MacKenzie. His second choice was Leo Durocher—both Franco-Americans, actually, but strangely close to my father in talents and temperament. That became another tribal extender: how did Boudreau do last night? Did Durocher win? We're a race of shortstops: Bressoud and Belanger. There are no giants here. When the great power-hitting outfielder André Dawson came up with the Montreal Expos, the local press was on it in a minute: André, André? He said he didn't think he was French.

But given a context, you can walk through these villages, sit by these lakes and on these mountaintops, read the parish ledgers glimpsing back hundreds of years, and still feel the resistance of an ancient god. The ruins can still feel like the dead Mogul cities on the jackalled plains of India or the oracular ruins at Delphi, these villages like Piopolis and the candlelit, crutch-lined shrines of Ste-Anne de Beaupré and the tomb of Brother André in Montréal under the spectacular dome of the Oratoire St-Joseph. North American relics of an absentee landlord, still extracting his tithe.

If I'm totally honest with myself, I'm sorry to see some of it—that ferocious old faith—go. Without it, for better and worse, there'd be no Black Robe, no French at all spoken on this continent. There's no theology quite like Pascal's, no evocation of the terrors of God like the Jansenists' and the Puritan divines', whatever corpse remains of their influence.

I THINK THIS IS WHAT APPEALS to part of me about being French-Canadian. We're so close to being the same as everyone else on this continent, yet so far away. We were the blue-eyed Chinese at the turn of the century. We're the oldest North Americans, yet the most separate. The most innocently imitative and the most fiercely self-protective. The most modern and European, the most secular, yet still deeply scarred by faith.

The lowest birth rate in North America. The most reluctant to admit immigrants. We're dying out.

These hills and lakes contain the part of me that I denied—my father's half—and that was denied to me. I am moved by the spectacle and the achievement of survival, of a remnant people not capitulating to overwhelming numbers and temptations. There is no way of knowing if any of its power is retrievable for me or even if it should be disturbed. I remember the lines in Gore Vidal's *Julian* ("The Apostate"), where the Romanized and Christianized emperor asks the last old pagan priestess, the *python,* if the ancient gods still spoke, if they should be restored. And she says no, the prophet-springs speak no more. That's what I had tried to do in moving my family to Montréal at the age of 26: wipe out my early history, be reborn. Start out again, this time right, without accident. The results were mixed.

A N D S O, at the base of a modern temple dedicated to the immeasurable and impersonal dimensions of time and space stands a decaying village consecrated to the most reactionary filaments of the faith. One hundred forty miles directly west, in Montréal, stands a third dome also on Pius IX Boulevard: Olympic Stadium, the crumbling, two-billion-dollar home of the Montreal Expos baseball team, the only indoor rain-making facility in the world. Infallibility ended there.

South and east of Piopolis the mountain ridges widen, clefts deepen, opening up one of the larger lakes in southeastern Québec, lac Mégantic, ten miles long and three miles wide, two hundred feet deep—the trapper of fishes—in the original Abenaki language. Unbridged and reasonably unexploited, looped by hills, forests, small towns, and a leisurely provincial road, the lake and the cottages on its shores seem to embody all that is traditional in the Québec landscape and character. A lake, a cottage, a boat. *Pêcher, communier, bricoler.*

Lac-Mégantic (the village takes the hyphen) is the largest town in the region called Frontenac, virtually a synonym for the back of beyond. The distances from large cities are not great—the scale is New Englandish—one hundred hard miles south of Quebec City and at least three hours on narrow roads east of Montréal, but here distance is measured in time not miles. Frontenac is still too long ago for modern *québécois.*

Nowadays, the sandy beaches are spotted with the modest cottages of the local petite-bourgeoisie. It looks peaceful, virtually unspoiled. The state of Maine lies just twenty miles east, over the mountains, and the moose-dense extrusion of northeastern New Hampshire a like distance south. It's all so tranquil, and so deceptive! It's tempting to imagine this blue lake with its sandy beaches and rolling, forested hills having no history. It's difficult to imagine the depth of family suffering this area has witnessed. It's hard to believe that Frontenac was frontier just a hundred years ago, that Mégantic is far newer than California, far younger than Iowa, where I now live. Fifty years ago, getting to Lac-Mégantic from Quebec City or Montréal was an achievement as unlikely as landing on the

Great Wall of China. Fathers would send postcards: *J'y suis, et je n'y reste plus!* (I'm here, and I'm getting out!)

Canada had spread to the Pacific before Lac-Mégantic was founded in 1885. The Blais family had been in the New World since Pierre Blais of Angoulême married Anne Perrot in 1669, but it took his tenant-farming descendants twelve generations to drift just one hundred miles south and to break their tenancy to the land. My grandfather was the first industrial worker, the first *journalier* in the family.

Ninety years ago when my aunts and uncles were death-marked children and my father not yet born, contiguous parts of Maine and Québec belonged to Ste-Agnès parish in Lac-Mégantic. The legal and psychological border between French Canada and French New England did not exist. (The families didn't recognize it, but the *New York Times* did; the terrors of French-Canadian immigration and the "Roman Catholic take-over of New England" inspired two of the *Times'* most racist editorials, which I'll quote later.) Families lapped over the edges of the border as they do today in Mexico and south Texas. When my father died, he was buried in what the aging locals called *le petit coin du Canada* (to give a flavor of the accent, "le p'tzee kwang dzu Canodo"—the little corner of Québec).

The first French word I learned from my father was one of his favorites: *coincé*. Cornered.

I feel nostalgia for this world I never saw, never knew. It was just a word, a blank for me to fill in—father's place of birth—or it was words, numbers, *undeuxtroisquatrecinq,* grunts and stutters that he added and subtracted. That's

French, I'd explain to my friends. "Elle-em" trees and movie "fill-ems"; was that French, or something regionally New England? His "blue," came out "blyew" the way crooners stretched it; but then, he'd been a singer and had taught himself proper American English from Bing Crosby records. In truth, he spoke neither language well. He'd forgotten much of his French and his normal English was profane: street-learned, word-poor, and musically fabricated.

I GREW UP with no legends of Québec, only with my mother's stories of Montréal in the thirties where priests merely patted the farebox as they got on buses and handsome police raided socialist meetings. It was an English-Canadian's Montreal—without the accent mark—charming and corrupt with a population to be pitied. My mother's best stories were of Manitoba and Saskatchewan and of London and pre-Hitler Germany where she'd studied, and Prague, where she'd worked. She made me yearn for her Canada, but when my parents divorced it was to Quebec City that I started hitchhiking, and it was French that I drove myself to learn though I never spoke a word of it to my father. I used French around him whenever he visited us in Montréal, trying to gain his approval. He always spoke in English and clung to the fiction that he was an American.

My fiction was that I was Canadian, and French at that.

Deprive a boy of a father and the boy will invent him. Deprive a boy of his community and he will seek it. Withdraw his father's presence and the boy will slowly fabricate him in his own image. My parents provided me with twenty-six potential aunts and uncles—seventeen from my father and nine from my mother—but left me, predictably, an only child.

Because my father had no friends, valued no friendships or commitments, denied his family, expressed no nostalgia, held nothing sacred, I have become a man of revisitations, sentiment, heritage, obligation, and letters. I've let nothing, and no one, go, from high school, college, or thirty cities afterwards. When he wasn't surrounded by strangers, buying them drinks, he'd be home, asleep. "Keep me company," he'd say to me or my mother. He said it years later in his hospital bed. If my father had not denied his origins, he might have doubted his own existence. My mother and I liked nothing better than solitude.

A secular mythology is at work here, the slow and inevitable transformation of the aging son into the dead father. The attempt of the grown man to finally take down the scaffolding of his work-in-progress and look, for once, in the mirror at his finished product. We never looked alike in my fair-skinned, allergenic, clumsy growing-up and in his olive-skinned, athletic prime, but I look now as I remember him in his fifties at the pinnacle of his Pittsburgh achievements. I was sixteen when he was my age now.

I SPENT THE MOST VIVID YEARS of my childhood in the swamps and lake country of central Florida in the late 1940s, two hundred miles northwest of Arthur Godfrey's daily broadcasts from Miami Beach. People said you could trust Arthur Godfrey. If you listened long enough you might hear him make fun of his sponsors. I remember my rage comparing the impoverished Florida I knew—the moss-pickers I went to school with, the worms in my feet that my mother treated with carbolic acid, and the worms she killed with dabs of acid on my rectum holding a flashlight as they churned out of my guts at night to spawn, the Ku Klux Klan (local politicians and businessmen who unmasked themselves every Confederate Memorial Day leading a cavalcade of convertibles with the high school band and beauty queens so we'd know who to vote for and where to shop)—with the packaged Tourist Board pap Arthur Godfrey was sending out on the airwaves. Talk about us, Frank Parker and Marian Marlowe and Haleloke! not about the warm breezes and the ocean waves. It was rage, my earliest rage, at the lies I heard every day about a world that infested every inch and every minute of my life. I was only eight or nine but I had a politics of resentment.

I think now that's the only politics my father ever had.

Like my father I was raised without electricity or running water, among illiterates. I fished for our family's food in the trapper of fishes known as Lake Harris. I played with migrant workers whose families numbered fifteen or more and whose children died and were buried almost without comment by the survivors. I remember those lakes flooding in hurricane season and depositing a film of dead fish as the waters retreated. I remember the alligators pulling themselves over the Florida Central tracks and old black porters tossing blocks of ice out the back car for us kids to fight over and bring home to our mothers.

Those lakes of central Florida have a potency for me that must have rivaled my father's memory of lac Mégantic where his father walked the logs in summer and skated in the winter extending his arms under a buffalo robe and billowing out of sight.

The memories laid down early are like the lakes and paths and creeks of the Florida landscapes I knew. And now they pool to the outline of their deepest and earliest depressions. The eight miles between Leesburg and Tavares at one time filled my entire life. I learned to bicycle on the deserted runways of my father's rented airport, which he had converted to a furniture factory. I named those runways my highways, invented destinations—California, New York—at the end of each runway. I thought of myself as a bus driver, and that's what I wanted to be when I grew up, a man who knew every building and could rattle off every town name in order.

A few years ago, when we were invited down to Gainesville for readings at the University of Florida, I brought my wife to that lakeside off Route 441 between Leesburg and Tavares, to the cabin still standing at the end of a sandy trail. I tried to explain the cougars in those woods, the snake trails across the sand ruts, the savannahs where the Dowdy boys and I would cut palmetto fronds to make arrows and cut up old inner tubes to make our bowstrings. The sights! The smells! The cuts and infections and tropical diseases! I'd written the better part of two story collections about that patch of sand and the people living on the shore, the terrors in that water. The lake is tame now, like Mégantic, devoid it seems of all history and suffering. Disney World infects the edges. The petite bourgeoisie of Leesburg and Tavares have tiny cabins at the water's edge. The old boat-landing where I used to fish is gone now, filled in. The old track bed is still raised like a gravel dike, but the tracks and ties are gone. A man in the sandy yard was repairing his pickup truck. The bumper sticker said:

I Don't Care How They Do It Up Nawth.

Like my father, I grew up in the backyard of tourist country with a hatred of all those who came our way in their big white cars, their strange clothes and accents, their expectations of a good time, their reinterpretation of our weather, our food, our quaint poverty. Out on the highway half a mile from the lake and the shack we lived in, up the sandy trail canopied in live oak, I sold little figurines I made from plaster of Paris poured into red rubber molds and painted with my mother's watercolors. I ingratiated myself to them, exaggerating my accent, and spitting watermelon seeds while they took pictures, and I dreamed of killing their children, little whiners crying for Cokes. Like my father I became a good salesman.

IN THE WINTER of my fifty-first year, at a jazz singer's loft party in Manhattan, I asked a young woman I'd been talking to where she was from. "Tavares, Florida," she answered, then catching my response, pressed forward. "What's wrong?" I established my Tavares credentials: the

Ku Klux Klan, the lakes, the worms in the feet (she was too young for any of it)—it was a strange conversation for Soho. Never, she explained later, does she answer anything but "Florida" to such cocktail chitchat. If pressed, to dispel the taint of Miami or Ft. Lauderdale, she might admit to Orlando. She never says Tavares to anyone. Nowadays, coincidences happen every day. I've run out of running room, my life and the outer world are dense with allusion.

Something about my attachment to geography elicits these precise responses. When I ask, as I always do, *where do you come from?* I mean to ask *who are you?* Or perhaps, to stick with the Neptune and Pluto analogy, my question can be further deconstructed: *Where do you come from?* really means *who am I?* If she hadn't have come from Tavares, Florida, what would I have talked about?

IN 1977, when my wife and I were living in New Delhi (she was serving as the Resident Director of a Canadian educational institute that year; I was writing a novel), I asked the American agricultural attaché at a Canadian party where he'd been born. "Fargo, North Dakota—almost a Canadian," he said, a little apologetically. "Well, so was I!" I admitted, "—almost an American." "What hospital?" he asked. "St. John's," I said. "Would you by any chance remember the name of your doctor?" he asked. "Dr. Hannah," I said. The man took a deep breath, then called his wife over. "This is the woman who delivered you," he said. "She was Dr. Hannah's delivery room nurse."

"A shame about Dr. Hannah, wasn't it?" she said.

Apparently, the doctor who had delivered me committed suicide many years later. I was thirty-seven in 1977, still on the outward voyage of my life. Meeting the hands that had welcomed me to the world, that had washed me off, at a cocktail party in India was the first great coincidence of my life. Maybe I had reached the outer limit of my private universe, the moment when everything, ever so slightly, begins curving back.

IF A TREE FELL in the forest and no one heard it, did a tree fall? If I had a grandfather whom I knew quite well, read about, and am said to resemble, and I had another grandfather whose name I had to learn, whose picture I never saw, who left me nothing in the way of stories or memories, could I be said to have had two grandfathers?

A WEEK AFTER THE PARTY in the Manhattan loft I was back in Leesburg and Tavares, invited down for a reading at Central Florida University in Orlando. My host-professor drove me up the twenty-five miles of super-highway to Leesburg, and I found my old house still standing on South Street. The street where we bicycled under the bug-dense lights until our mothers called us in for sleep is paved now and the lot we cleared and played baseball on is walled off, hiding a retirement compound. My side of the street is unchanged.

An old lady, chewing tobacco and sitting with her grandchild on the old verandah where I read comic books and studied maps while fine dust drifted through the house, reminisced about the neighborhood that she'd known since 1953. Only since 1953? I predated her in the house by six years. I'm the pioneer here, the old Cracker, despite appearances.

When I was a child, Big Mama English, a hundred years old in 1947, lived next door, and she remembered Yankee troops. My Big Mama had been a teenager, a belle, in the Civil War, older even than my mémère who'd been born in 1865. Ancient history had surrounded me, growing up. The Big Mama of 1992, with her chaw and her cleated teeth, denies my memories of a goldfish pond in the backyard by the laundry house where turtles devoured the fishes, of a stone wall between our houses where mockingbirds pulled snakes from the crevices and shook them till they died. "I bin here since nineteen and fifty-three," she proudly insists. "Ain't never bin none of that." Spit, chew. She denies the savagery of my southern childhood, the nights I spent sleeping over with friends, the incest I witnessed, the kerosene and sugar I was obliged to swallow whenever I coughed.

I used to stock that goldfish pond, buying new fish every couple of weeks. It was a revelation to me that birds were stronger than snakes, or that one frog could clean out a fishpond overnight, or that turtles could even stir themselves sufficiently to catch a fish. Or that fish could be so slow, or stupid, as to get caught by tadpoles, frogs, and turtles.

When I was eight years old, I was struck on the jaw by a batted baseball while playing in the vacant lot, a reclaimed marsh, across the street. I was rushed from Leesburg to the only dentist in the region, in Orlando. I had become a Cracker, a Florida native. As an inducement against the pain of being wired up, I was told that his office was three stories high. I could ride an elevator and look out on the whole state of Florida while he worked on my jaw. Orlando had ten thousand people, an immense figure. It seemed like a dark, brooding, northern city full of sky-scrapers and elevators. The idea of a university in my old region of swamps and disease is alternately heroic and comic.

I want to own central Florida imaginatively, just as I have wanted to own Pittsburgh and Montréal in my life, and I cannot. Those places are cut-off segments of my life, appropriate only to the '40s, '50s, and '70s. I come from nowhere, I live nowhere, my future is noplace. I want to reverse the flow of tourists and retirement villages, bring back the mudfish and panthers, the pestilence and super-stition, that old-time religion and Jansenism.

THE NOVEL I WAS WRITING that year in New Delhi is called *Lunar Attractions*. It begins with a strong evocation of a central-Florida childhood, especially the house in Lees-burg and the life of that dusty street. The mother has a spontaneous abortion in the laundry house out back. The boy digs in a dry ditch and finds a buried mudfish, which he connects with all the losses in his life. In short, I own that street, that house, and that backyard, imaginatively.

Several years later the opportunity arose to write an introduction to a reissue of that book, and I remembered with rueful pleasure the sensual ease with which that Flor-ida book was handwritten from a New Delhi bedroom.

At the time I hadn't seen Florida in twenty-five years, and politically it was as distant as it has ever been. (I was a Montréal-based Canadian at the time.) Then, I consulted an atlas.

Delhi and Leesburg are on precisely the same latitude, twenty-nine degrees north, and at exactly the same minute. In other words, the light was the same. Lizards on the walls of our Delhi flat became the Florida alligators of my memory. Especially suggestive was the hour or two of echoed heat and daylight in the subtropical summer twilight, the magic hours of peach-tinted skies when children rode their bikes after an early dinner. In India, I would walk out behind our glass-enclosed, architect-designed house, across the open field where our upscale "colony" dumped its trash. In that field, pariah dogs fed, families of ragpickers extracted usable cloth, and trashpickers stuffed old papers into jute sacks.

(In the central Florida I was writing about, the moss-picker families—the Dowdys, who lived in the open-faced shanties at the water's edge—would twist their hooked poles into the Spanish moss, pull it down and quickly stuff it into jute sacks. They were paid ten cents a hundred-weight for the bug-infested moss that would be rubberized and used as furniture stuffing. I helped out, but the chigger bites got to be too much to handle.)

The open field abutted a brick wall dating back to Mogul times. Families had carved sleeping perches into the wall. A few entrepreneurs ran tire-patching stalls or cigarette kiosks under lean-tos tied to the wall. Goats wandered the narrow streets, children kicked a soccer ball, the older boys had made a cricket-pitch on the field of trash.

The village was not more than half a kilometer from an upper middle-class modern Delhi suburb, but it could have existed precisely as it did without Delhi's presence. Half a kilometer of distance equaled a hundred years of time. It was a handy metaphor of human memory. Florida was crashing in on me then, just as Québec is now. In those walks, I would plan the next day's writing. Images had never come more fluently; I couldn't wait for each day's writing to begin. I saw my next twenty novels laid out before me—I wasn't yet aware that my universe had reached its outer limit. I had merely reentered a band of light, a quality of thin heat, odors of rot, and veils of mosquitoes that I hadn't known in thirty years. It hasn't happened since. The memory is heliotropic.

When my whole life was contained in that stretch of Route 441 between Leesburg and Tavares and my sense of the urban character was built around visits to Orlando and especially the visits of the Orlando Giants to Venetian Gardens, where the Leesburg Pirates played, and my mother would say, "Their boys are so much bigger and older than ours, it's not fair," I read maps like novels. Cities were the important characters, the obvious heroes and heroines of a country. Major cities gathered highways in their fists like stagecoach drivers with horses' reins. They hogged the best harbors and the junctions of the major rivers. Little cities with elevations and populations far larger than anything I knew in Florida (Atlanta and Pittsburgh were, by then, distant memories) were forced to serve them. They'd been captured in a gravity they couldn't escape. Losers in a close game. I scanned the maps for twin cities, seeing in them instances of myself, a desire for proximity but a fear of absorption, and read into their placement not a spillover of tract housing, ethnicities, or looser moralities—the Phenix City and Covington complex—but a sad plot of competition and capitulation. The strong and the weak, the cruel and the virtuous, the husband-cities with their busy ring of wife and children suburbs.

The events in our lives, the places we've been and the people we've known, keep coming back. Our life is one long novel and as we work our way through the second half it's small wonder we never escape those crucial first pages, when the light was set for all time, when the world was an intimate place, and all its inhabitants were known by name. They were all at the dance and they got their hands stamped on the way out. They can wander back without paying, without warning, any time they want.

MY PARENTS WERE BOTH BORN to homesteaders on separate Canadian frontiers. In each case, the towns grew up around them. My mother, the oldest of ten, was born in Wawanesa, Manitoba, in 1903 to the Shakespeare-quoting, Ontario-born town doctor and his landlady's daughter. He was a graduate of the first medical class of the University of Manitoba; he is the good grandfather, the one I know about, the bald one I resemble. They called him the Luther Burbank of Canada because of his interest in crossbreeding Ontario and Chinese fruit trees and adapting them for growth in western Canada. The one who held me a few months after my birth in 1940 and said to my mother, "Don't worry, Annie, this boy will never be a boxer." (I didn't walk till I was nearly four, or speak until I was three and a half.) Five generations of my mother's family have graduated from the University of Manitoba, and my mother is buried with her parents in Winnipeg—talk about rooted! The last three of those generations have died of Alzheimer's disease.

MY PARENTS ARE BURIED in the towns they lived in the longest and thought they had fled. The city I've lived in longest is Montréal, but on that winter weekend in Orlando and Leesburg I told my host-professor that if I died that day, to bury me there. It still speaks. I remembered all the streets and suddenly I stood at a pay phone and flipped through the flimsy phone book and my classmates' names from forty-five years ago blossomed in my brain. Pilkington! Chapman! Anderson! Stanridge! Davis!

NOWADAYS WITH EXOGENY SO COMMON that everyone it seems is half Jewish, Asian, Black, or Hispanic (and it's often the less exotic half), it's hard to imagine that the differences in my parents' backgrounds were as great as anything ever established among whites on this continent. My mother thought of it as an intermarriage. It earned her temporary banishment from the family, and only provisionary acceptance for the rest of her life. The French to the English-Canadians were a *race* before they became a *nation*. Canada in the 1930s was a vast and sluggish Northern Ireland, opposing solitudes of self-righteousness, meeting only on the sides of cereal boxes.

And, of course, I married even more exogenously than my parents. Nothing in my background prepared me or them for a Hindu wife. Like my father, I married above my station, socially and educationally. Like him, my father-in-law is in *Who's Who*. I, who grew up ignorant of my origins and slightly afraid of what I might find, but who memorized maps and geographies as though they were secret languages, married into a confident and wealthy family who knew its origins for all time—they are Brahmins, sprung from the head of God. And from a place, Calcutta, that conjured only fear, that I'd never visited, never thought about, and knew nothing of. Nothing.

Before we married in a lunch-hour civil ceremony thirty years ago, my wife received a wire from her father hoping to avert disaster: "Get his horoscope." She was marrying the son of a twice-divorced (at the time), unemployed one-time boxer, liquor-runner, wife-beater, and furniture salesman. She might have said accurately enough (calling out the Indian air force or a team of kidnappers in the process): *He is the grandson of illiterate sharecroppers.* Both my fathers—my in-law and my outlaw—are dead now, but this book is partially that horoscope I was afraid to send thirty years ago.

CHAPTER FOUR

I AM IN WELLINGTON, New Zealand. It is a brisk late-
summer Sunday, the middle of March 1992, with gale force
winds crashing like thunder on the hotel windows. At four
A.M. the streets below are empty. The motorway behind
the hotel is deserted; two taxis pass in twenty minutes. In
all that concrete and mercury-vapored emptiness, the tree-
tops toss dementedly. Outside it looks and sounds like a
hurricane, but the streets are dry. I am trying to convey
confusion, although it may sound like smug opportunism.
Travel is my professional medium; it is indispensable to
what I do for a living. I am an arts administrator at the
University of Iowa; I bring writers from all over the world
to Iowa City.

My life is like the Hellenic Empire. I cover the known
world, thin as dust. The reader can make the logical connection between my travels as a child, and these mighty
leaps I make as an adult. The atlas of my childhood has
come alive; my life is an atlas. The previous paragraph was
written in New Zealand. This paragraph was written in
Buenos Aires two weeks later.

On the flight to New Zealand, I ate my United Airlines meals but left the dessert. I always leave the dessert.
The meal is complete and satisfactory only when a dessert

is presented that I can reject. If the dessert had not been presented, I would have felt hungry and deprived. It is a kind of post-modern dessert then, satisfying for its unsampled presence, for having signified dessertness. Dessertality. I want my father for dessert, even if I don't eat him.

I have never watched or listened to the in-flight movie. It signifies flight and movement but is an unsatisfactory example of itself, that is, as cinema. (My older son, a film cameraman, often says, with justice, "We work our asses off pulling focus and mastering hundreds of shots and lighting techniques so it can be reduced, blurred, and shown on a plane?") Without it, however, I would not feel I was on a serious, life-enhancing flight. I would feel cheated, and I would demand they plan other distractions for me, which I could also reject.

In other words, the little creme bar with the chocolate icing and the in-flight movie, *Curly Sue,* both hold clues to me about my father. He is a meta-father, a concept of fatherness. Fatherality. My problem, if you haven't guessed it yet, is that I am a meta-self at times, a construct of pieces adding up to a self, even to the person writing this.

One afternoon in Iowa City last year, I took in a movie. An old couple sat behind me; we were otherwise alone together. The trailer-ad was for a ballet movie called *Dancing with Your Feet,* with ample teasers of soft-focus dances through golden wheat fields, and star-names that could have been Australian or British—Jessica and Natalia and Shawn—all convincingly balletmaniacal. "Oh, I want to see this!" whispered the old lady to her husband. Then suddenly from the corner of the screen came the Eveready pink rabbit, banging his drum. The dancers stopped and stared. "Still going!" chimed the announcer.

"What was that?" the woman cried. "That rabbit came right through the middle of the movie!"

"Damnedest thing I ever saw," said her husband. "They must have scrambled the reels."

And now, I wanted to turn and say to them, *you'll never know until it's over if you've been jerked around or not.* It's post-modernism. A pink rabbit transforms the footage; the parody is not in the material, it comes from outside and casts everything in a retrospective absurdity. And not just that: even if it doesn't appear, it projects an anticipated absurdity over everything yet to come.

When you don't watch television and you see the pink rabbit for the first time, it must be a shock. You must feel, for an instant (until you muster a familiar defense: *they must have switched the reels, incompetent young fools probably high on drugs up in the projection booth*) that the world has been changed on you, that from this moment on, you will be incompetent to judge what you are seeing. In fact, you will no longer be allowed to trust your own senses. I felt this way after my parents divorced, and in subtler ways, I feel it today. Life had passion and meaning so long as they were together. Then it became a joke.

Go home, old man.

I AM IN NEW ZEALAND for a Festival of the Arts, where my wife is one of the featured American writers. It's an opportunistic visit—I can negotiate for my Iowa program with the Queen Elizabeth II Arts Council for a New Zealand author, while meeting a few dozen world authors during a week of readings and parties. In terms of my ongoing identity-search, I can say with confidence: I'm not exactly a Nobody, but I'm not quite a Somebody.

Literary eminences from all over the writing world are here—Americans like Alice Walker, Oliver Sacks, and Bharati Mukherjee—major world voices like Orhan Pamuk, Philip Salom, Ivan Klíma, and Daniela Crasnaru. Some had launched their international presence in the program I now direct at Iowa. The talk is of the festivals we've attended—Finland, Adelaide, Toronto, Budapest, San Francisco, London, Singapore, Vancouver, and Iowa. The palaces in Prague and Italy. The gossip concerns the bitches and bastards among us, the menacing sharks and playful dolphins. We all know each other ("Salman sends his greetings"), where to eat and where to stay in every city of the world. The army of airborne writers moves across the world like the professional golf or tennis tour hitting all the Opens. At our worst, we're turning into characters from a David Lodge novel. It's lovely while it lasts—shy and private people being fêted as celebrities—and in Wellington crowds turn out by the hundreds for every reading and panel discussion, but I fear it's a bubble about to burst, like the overheated paperback market in the United States a few years ago.

Thirty years ago, no one had ever met a non-exhibitionistic writer. I went all the way to Harvard to study for a summer when I heard Bernard Malamud, the writer I most admired, was actually teaching. Now, any interested undergraduate in America has met too many.

We're everywhere. The only lasting celebrity, like United Airlines desserts, is in trying to remain untouched.

ON THE DAY I leave New Zealand, terrorists blow up the Israeli Embassy in Buenos Aires. The apartment we'll be staying in had all its windows blown out. If we'd been drinking tea in the living room, we would have been slashed by flying glass.

Later that same day, thanks to gaining a day on the international date line, I'm back in the office in Iowa City. Off the plane in time to teach my graduate seminar. Before my lecture on *Schindler's List,* I get a call from a writer in Peru who hopes to join the program in the fall. He's just survived the fourth attempt on his life by the Shining Path revolutionaries. I tell him I'm going to Argentina in a few hours. "Be very careful," he counsels, "it's dangerous down there."

"The Embassy bombing?" I ask.

"No, no, amigo. The cholesterol. All the red meat and all the red wine. Very dangerous."

TIME TO DISCUSS my own indiscretions. I am deeply unfaithful in perhaps a unique way. I spent the Wellington week excusing myself from readings and literary interviews, sneaking into real estate offices and looking at properties. New Zealand speaks to me. I have been reading New Zealand novels and stories, a book of essays called *Pakeha: The quest for identity in New Zealand.* Other people's identity problems are confections to me; my world is an

aquarium of exotic creatures all without fixed identity. We
are like the soft meat of hermit crabs, forever shedding
shells and desperately looking for any older, larger, used
one to crawl into before some predator seizes us.

I want always to change, to rewrite my codes, to alter
everything about myself. Passports, accent, schools,
hometowns. Places seduce me. In my life, as these pages
will soon make clear, I've just about run out of hometowns
and passports and places to have come from. Each move
is like an affair, a change of air, a lightness of step, a clean
slate, and a fresh start. I am not an exile forced to change
residences as a matter of survival; I'm more a barnacle
hitching a ride.

At a reception for the Canadian writers attending the
New Zealand Festival thrown by the Canadian High Commission, I talked like a Winnipeg native with the High
Commissioner—after all, my mother and grandparents are
buried in Winnipeg, and I went to school there. He's a
Winnipegger and an old friend of my uncle's family. He
knows my aunts and cousins, he has been on our family
farm. A few hours earlier I'd paid a courtesy call to the
American Embassy and ended up talking like a Pittsburgher—after all, I graduated from high school there—
with the cultural attaché. A few hours later at a publisher's
party, I spent the evening talking in French with a woman
whose child was fathered by a French-Canadian, because,
after all, I'd spent my happiest and most productive years
in Montréal. There were no Floridians, no Cincinnatians,
no Torontonians at the parties to chew over streets and
classmates with, but there were Bengalis to take us around
at night and, after all, I've been married to Calcutta for

thirty years, written a book on it, and immersed myself in its totality as a way of becoming a satisfactory husband.

It's a sickness, this chameleon-nature, this relationship that is practically sexual with the locations of the world, a promiscuity of place and not with people. I don't pick up women; I pick up hometowns. I don't have conquests; I have cities-I-have-known and felt at home in, gone to school in, explored, loved.

MY FATHER LIED to everyone about his origins. My mother would leave the room when he started in: the Paris birth, the Harvard education, the vast family he supported . . .

GIVE ME TWO DAYS in most places and I see myself absorbing the grid, the newspapers, the television, tramping the neighborhoods, trying to impose belonging. Learning new sports. On New Zealand television, Test Match cricket is playing, and I watch until I can understand the terminology, the high numbers, the skill, and the strategy. The visiting British cricket team is in our hotel; up close they're huge, they're major league. America: cricket's great. Cricket counts.

My hosts in Argentina are old cricketers, Anglo-Argentines with perfect British accents whose families have been "in the Argentine" for over a hundred years. It's another kind of subculture, a perfectly bilingual Planter society. With no family ties to Britain, with all their relatives scattered throughout South America, my hosts and friends switch from Spanish to English un-consciously, checking only my blank reaction before apol-ogizing and switching back. It's another kind of identity confusion, one of the most complicated and textured to be found anywhere. They are of British stock, these expert cattle ranchers and grain farmers; the Latin tem-perament is respected so far as it goes, but faintly dis-trusted. But the grandchildren are all Spanish-speaking. One son teaches in Nicaragua. The tight vessel is rup-turing.

We sip the local wine, lift ribs and sausage and chops from the fire. The houses are old, cool and high-ceilinged, ranged under groves of elm and eucalyptus. Vistas open out on manicured lawns, English gardens and the grassy fields dotted with Angus herds. The scale is out of Africa, the particulars minutely English. These are unrecon-structed squires and settlers, Reaganite Tories, they can't conceive of a principled opposition like Labour or the Democrats. We talk instead of memorable local cricket matches, famous local love affairs, for these are salty ("Dickie was always bothering the girls, wasn't he? Mummy told him once to go fuck a spider"), hearty, ro-bust, worldly people, enormously generous with hospi-tality, with gossip, with tales.

It's another form of time-travel. I can imagine the noble Sieurs from Old France, surveying their rocky acreage in Québec, living a version of the same life, and holding much the same attitudes, or the slave-holding American planters who welcomed de Tocqueville, or even a modern Afrikaner, throwing *braatjes* on the grille for an inquisitive guest.

French-Canadians are Afrikaners without the race laws.

The Buenos Aires apartment, central and furnished, is ours to use for the asking. Yesterday, the country and the city was a literary void (as only Borges can make it seem); today, we've tramped the streets, called on old Argentine friends, gone to dinner, had drinks, made courtesy calls on foundations, and even been interviewed by the local papers: B.A. has become a dense and satisfying experience. I see myself coming down for a month or two, studying intensive Spanish, mingling with the crowds. Being *porteño*.

I SEE MY PARENTS' MARRIAGE now as a kind of clash of colonialities. The French-Canadians, a garrison mentality, afraid to venture forth, suspicious of outsiders, always defensive about the loss of language, culture, and religion. Tenacious people, surviving three hundred years on the shoulder of an English-speaking, Protestant continent.

My mother was a colonial product, but a guilty colonial, in rebellion against her background, skeptical of Britain, religion, and the Crown. She was determined to do something with her education beyond using it to land a good husband (her father's idea). And so, after a B.A. and teaching degree from Wesley College (now University of Winnipeg), she taught three years in Saskatchewan and Manitoba villages (Guernsey, Dauphin), saved her wages, and sailed on to Europe in 1930 to get an art education. Her father would not pay for such foolishness. She went to Germany, took in lectures at the Bauhaus, and left in 1933 for Prague when the Nazis closed down culture.

Colonial confidence gave my mother her bravery and her sense of mission among the benighted French and the vulgar Americans. She was a calamity of literacy and liberalism in my father's life, introducing his only child to art and books and away from anything crude or violent. She saw in my father an unpolished gem, and she thought she could bring out his good qualities (those were her words to me, repeated on dozens of occasions right up to the final moments of her marriage, "Lee has his good qualities . . . Lee struggles to do the right thing . . . Lee can't help himself, poor man").

In my mother's decency there was always the streak of unconscious condescension. "Poor things," she'd say of natives of any country, of the local blacks, of ill-kept animals of any sort. Anne, too, tried to do the right thing, and she had far more than a few good qualities. But the fact that I am writing this book about my father and not my mother is a sign that if I had followed *le chemin de ma mère* I would have turned out too much the good boy, the good, untwisted man, the Good Colonial.

CHAPTER FIVE

I WAS BORN with a condition that kept me crib-bound for my first three years and never let me catch up, physically, with the great baboon-troop of boyhood and adolescence. The original diagnosis, *amytonia congenita,* is invariably fatal, which gives a sense of its gravity and my mother's desperation in finding a cure. I couldn't lift my head and I didn't speak, but she never abandoned the belief that I would recover and lead a normal life. The disability, if that's what it was (later doctors simply called it a mysterious dystrophy), amounted in later life to pudginess, slowness, and an occasional thyroid collapse that would send me to bed for months on end while my body spread like pudding. All the running I do merely keeps me stout instead of obese.

I'd call it now a malleability factor. Without muscle tone, I also lacked firm ligaments and tendons. I could twist my body into any shape, legs around my neck, fingers bent backwards, feet splayed out, or in, more than ninety degrees. When I finally began to speak, I was the miracle in my mother's life—her reason for living as she often said. It's as though we're born with a fixed number of good breaks and bad ones—millions of them—randomly arranged and randomly appearing. Like genes, on any particular day, they might line up fatally. Except for her and a lucky visit to a sympathetic and knowledgeable doctor in Cincinnati when I was three and had broken one of my glass-thin bones, I'd be dead or institutionalized today. We survive thousands of close calls before the one that finally takes us.

My mother was thirty-seven when I was born. I was the first child from her only marriage, which she must have known already was a disaster. I could have been taken as the confirmation; instead, she made me her trophy. She never ceased reading to me, clipping pictures, hanging maps, playing records. Thanks to thyroid extracts, I began scooting about the apartment, crab-like, then speaking, and finally, at four, taking my first steps. Many years later a doctor mentioned that I'd survived only because I was the first-conceived; her next five pregnancies were spontaneously aborted. My parents were profoundly incompatible—an Rh blood factor (which makes me doubt that my father had other children)—but, despite appearances and temperament, I am a fighter: Baby Clark, son of Kid Leo, the boxer.

The effect of my dystrophy was rubbery limberness. I was the raw mass out of which a body and personality would form, a kind of three-year-old fetus. I would sit in my high chair, legs wrapped around my neck, arms out on the tray. I rolled like a ball, legs tucked around my neck, arms free for paddling and steering. My fingers bent all the way back. (Even into high school I had trouble opening a car door—those chrome push buttons simply bent my thumb back rather than yielded as I applied pressure.)

Once I learned the alphabet, I began spelling words

with my fingers and body. I could flop and twist my fingers, my legs, into any shape, and I could spell words with a kind of spasmodic movement that was, according to cousins, truly revolting to watch. This, coupled with a helpless memorization of all the shapes of states and provinces, and their capitals, led to my first brush with fame.

Winnipeg, 1945. World War II was not yet over, and we went back from Pittsburgh to visit my grandparents. My father had just quit Sears and had decided to strike out on his own to Atlanta. Each of our major moves, each change of identity and possible destiny, was punctuated with a return to Canada, a few weeks or months of bliss, living with relatives in my grandfather's house. The trip to Winnipeg was perhaps my mother's long farewell, or maybe a last chance to save her soul; I was not part of that debate.

I remember standing with my uncle (the man who would later become a television star in Winnipeg, the head of the Wheat Pool, and friend of the eventual Canadian High Commissioner to New Zealand; nothing in the universe is ever lost), a colonel in his green woolen uniform and jaunty beret, watching a solar eclipse through smoked glass. My girl-cousins, athletic twins from Moose Jaw, did somersaults around the house.

The veteran's hospitals were full of wounded. It was thought the maimed and bedridden would get a kick out of a protoplasmic walking haystack, a child who could spell out answers and names with twists of his hands and body. Freak to freak. My aunts and mother took me down to a veteran's hospital to show me off, to answer geography questions by spelling them out, by spelling different words with my fingers while forming shapes with my body. Girlfriends' names and little messages: I was a human tattoo.

"That's how you become knighted, entertaining the troops," she said, igniting a fire that would burn for years. Sir Clark. One officious cousin reminded my mother I'd been born in North Dakota. I was a Yank, I couldn't become a Sir, and it pained me. Deprived of a family, deprived of cousins—the post-modern equivalents of brothers and sisters—deprived of all the accouterments of civilization—like a Union Jack and portraits of the King. We were Americans, though I never really accepted it: peerage-deficient.

Limber in body, rigid in ambition. Just a few months ago, unpacking a box in Iowa City, I found a sheaf of my father's old Atlanta letterheads: "Lee R. Blaise Show-rooms. We Cover Dixie" with a map of the South, Shreve-port to Richmond. The lettering in red, the map in blue. This is the little showroom he'd opened after we left Win-nipeg. The map is far more exact than it need be—my father was as keen on geography as I was, and it seems obvious to me now that geography became obsessive with me because he'd mastered it. It was, like baseball and fish-ing, a safe way for him to communicate.

Atlanta is where I started school. We lived in a rented room in the back of an East Point house: a bedroom, with a shared kitchen and bath. I slept in a corner of the kitchen. In Atlanta, my mother took me to my first movie, *Song of the South,* an object-lesson for racial instruction. The buses were air-conditioned, I drank Vernor's Ginger Ale and carried Toddle House hamburgers to my parents at work. Budd Aluminum's "Train of Tomorrow" came to Atlanta, and I caught the excitement of streamlined futurity. Cars, locomotives, buses—everything had to have that straining-at-the-finish-line thrust, that nose-first lunge to it, or else it wasn't modern. I started designing trains on endless sheafs of my father's letterhead. All I remember of the Atlanta house is the back garden where Olive, the house-owner's little girl my age, Big Daddy, her tubercular grandfather, and I picked blackberries. One day, I watched a mosquito land on my hand, and I didn't swat it. Seconds later a welt appeared; it was the first conscious link of cause and effect in my life. Years later, I tested positive for TB exposure.

There's nothing remarkable in my six-year-old artwork, except for the choice of subject—trains, cars, ships. The remarkable thing for me today is the signature of a six-year-old: *Clark L. Blaise (1940–   )*. If I am to believe the evidence, I had a middle initial and a sense of mortality, not to mention a grave little museum-quality ambition, by the time I started school. That could only have come from my mother.

IN THE LAST DAYS of 1986, during a move from Iowa City to New York, while unpacking boxes of books that had lain in storage for several years, I uncovered a slim, discolored volume entitled *The Borderland and Other Poems*, by a certain Roger Quin, "poet and bohemian" (b. 1850). The book is a reprint (Galashields and Son, Edinburgh, c. 1910) of an even more obscure first edition. The discoloring comes from smoke, a reminder of our disastrous house fire in Montréal in 1973. Only a few books and manuscripts, nothing else, survived that fire. Books purchased before the fire and preserved through two dozen moves since are signs of a certain commitment. I had probably purchased Quin's book at a church rummage sale in rural Québec in the mid-sixties.

For the Scots, border consciousness is a bardic art. That invisible, near-mythical Scottish border is a primeval literary marker, and the prototype for the border that obsesses me. I'm not Scottish and have never set foot in Scotland, but at one time in my life the thought of such a border spoke to me, as it would to many Canadians.

Anything to do with borders speaks to me personally. Crossing the border is like ripping the continent, an act of defiance, tearing its invisible casing. Borders are zones of grace, fifty miles wide on either side, where dualities of spirit are tolerated and commonplace. Around 1912 or so my father first pierced the American border, landing in Maine among his own relatives.

From a lifetime of crossing borders, I have developed a border consciousness. Borders mean metamorphosis, personal transformation. Borders demand decision, definition, but border-crossers are identity-smugglers, keeping a bland face, denying their purchases, waiting fifty miles to show their flag, unpack their goods.

Borders offer the opportunity to be opposing things without deception. I'm an American who writes fiction in Canada; a Canadian who writes essays in America. My father was a French criminal in Canada, an American Rotarian in Pittsburgh. I suppose I'm not alone, sensing the pull of a weak alien gravity, but I'm aware of its absurdity (Canada?) as well. Most Canadians in America have burrowed as far into the toes of the continent as they can get, south Florida and southern California. Borders are jurisdictions, signaling speedtraps and taxbreaks. For the well-adjusted, Canada is a different area code, nothing more.

Here is what the maladjusted, the unadjusted see:

Growing up in a map-strewn apartment in central Florida, I saw countries as bodies, and borders as their skin. Personalities grew out of shapes, and I responded to their outlines the way salesmen do to faces. Sri Lanka will never be other than a frozen drop of nectar, a punctuation of sorts to the funnel shape of India. From countries I went to states, and from states to counties: I read the clustering of counties like X-rays, knowing from their shapes where the populations were heavy or light, where the rivers and mountains were. While I was making those plaster-of-Paris

Indian figures and painting them with my mother's water-colors, I was also painting the states with all their counties, memorizing the county-seats, then cutting them up, freeing them from their states and learning to recognize ever smaller shapes, and pasting them on my walls like leaded glass. Then I made up my own shapes, my own counties and continents.

There was drama and personality in all the colored outlines. Vermont embraced New Hampshire in their rocky slice of rectangle. I approved the tentacular, surreptitious handshake of West Virginia and Maryland, snaking over Virginia and sliding under broad, uncomplicated Pennsylvania. The treachery of Gettysburg is no surprise, not to a map-reader with a sense of plot. The same with Pakistan and China, sneaking over the top of India and lightly touching fingers. There's disloyalty in the dagger thrust of West Virginia into the Union latitudes of Ohio and Pennsylvania. (Years later, my route home to Pittsburgh from college took me across that narrow strip of West Virginia, whose legacies were still preserved in fading "colored/white" motel signs.) Tennessee and North Carolina appeared as a sliced earthworm—two separate bodies from a single diagonal cut. I inferred hostility between Mississippi and Alabama, as they turned their backs on each other, like Siamese twins in a funk. Arizona and New Mexico did the same. Arkansas was a chipped flowerpot, Louisiana an overstuffed armchair, Minnesota a snake's stretched mouth about to ingest stupid, bovine Wisconsin. I liked broad, smiling Iowa, with its bulging cheek. What chrystalline compulsion of the universe accounts for the twinning of inanimate objects—why did Missouri and

Georgia take on similar shapes, even to tiny nipples at their southeast corners? Alberta and British Columbia were bloated versions of Nevada and California. The Yukon mimicked Idaho, and Montana played the American version of the Northwest Territories. Canada stooked its western provinces vertically like stacks of wheat, while the western states were boxes, cut square for stacking.

There's something morally and geographically proper about libertine Nevada rubbing up the backside of Mormonical Utah. And in my childhood, I took ancestral pride in the moral grandeur of one Canadian province, Ontario, doing the work of eight American states in keeping a lid on the Great Lakes.

American books, but not Canadian, seemed to end at the border. How could Americans complain of the bitter cold of the Dakotas, the rocky barrenness of New England, thinking themselves on the fringes of the universe, when adjacent regions in Canada were our warmest and most fertile? I loved Faulkner's sense of Canada, his use of Shreve McCannon, Quentin Compson's Harvard roommate, as the implied audience to the greatest of all American novels (for me), *Absalom, Absalom!* It's Shreve who asks the major question in the book and in Faulkner's writing—"Why do you hate the South?"—and it's to Shreve, a Calgarian, that Quentin cries his response: "I don't!" At one time, I made something of that formulation: the Southerner and the Canadian, back-to-back brothers (one gulping wide to ingest the Caribbean, Canadians coughing out the Arctic islands), with the belt of individualist, ahistorical Yankeeland in between. The only other American author with a consistently continental sense of origins, where criminals and detectives kept on going north without a sense of border was Ross Macdonald, and he, of course, was an old Canadian.

That borderless sense of borders, that ever-fluid deck of definitions, is my material.

There is, I think, a border mentality, just as there is a small-country mentality (*pace* Milan Kundera), or an exile mentality, a ghetto mentality, a garrison mentality, a planter mentality, an imperialist mentality, an island mentality. The border mentality is alert to differences, to calculating loss and advantage. It knows the exchange rates, it calculates in its head. It is adept at disguise and self-deception. It serves one master, profits from another, and fundamentally doesn't know who or what it is.

And there is a border mentality that can take liberty with borders as they are drawn and that seeks to arrange things more coherently. I was inspired, in a *Paris Review* interview, to read Carlos Fuentes' literary reinvention of the world. There is, for Fuentes, a Caribbean literature, subversive of history and language, a multilingual literature of history's castaways: "There is a culture of the Caribbean...that includes Faulkner, Carpentier, García Márquez, Derek Walcott, and Aimé Césaire [and to which I'd add Wilson Harris, Anthony Winkler, and V. S. Naipaul], a trilingual culture in and around the whirlpool of the baroque which is the Caribbean, the Gulf of Mexico."

And what do we make of Québec, I wonder, lacking a convenient metaphorical whirlpool (the Gulf of St. Lawrence?), yet which is no less a receptacle of the baroque, of defeated cultures and spent ideas, an intellectual reservation where Jansenism survived until the mid–20th century?

SOME BORDERS ARE CAGES, others are mirrors. Some purely political borders rasp on our consciousnesses—the various Koreas and Irelands and, until recently, the Germanys and South African "homelands." They seem to defy the common meaning of border, which is to define differences—these are borders that separate likenesses. Traditional borders, as in Europe, are natural reminders of where ancient armies ran out of steam, where languages and religions thinned out and faltered. Within the shell of a traditional border, it doesn't matter how small the country is: it defines the world. Other borders are aesthetic or cultural, such as that of Scotland, or the Mason-Dixon line, or dozens of others with poetic and psychological potency—the various *Gaeltaecht* regions of Ireland, the Breton, Welsh, Basque, Kurdish borders that exist only as maintained, and sometimes bloody, fictions. There are borders made of the thinnest membrane, such as that between Canada and the United States, which is undefended because it is maintained psychologically; the two sides have reached a mental stasis.

Borders are a supreme fiction. For the once-colonized, newly liberated, borders are a deformity; they create monsters. They do not define or protect, they do not express a collective will. They exacerbate instability. Borders are asylum walls, they separate natural brothers, they enclose natural enemies.

It took a psychic insurrection for V. S. Naipaul—to cite merely the best-known of the world's identity-torn consciousness—to declare his freedom from the accidental quadrant of his birth, the West Indies. His colonially determined birth as an uprooted Hindu in a Caribbean barracoon propelled him to Britain at the earliest date. A helpless, powerless colonial outpost like Trinidad, and a transplanted minority within it like the Indian Hindus, their myth-structure rendered absurd by transplantation, creates one kind of treachery, one kind of loyalty. A garrison mentality—survival at all costs—like Québec's, or Afrikanerdom's, or Israel's—creates something different. Desertion of the garrison in wartime—and it is always wartime in a garrison state—is a capital crime.

Writers like Naipaul—and there are dozens now, in England, Canada, and the United States, including the woman I have lived with for nearly thirty years—are psychologically several hundred years old. Born on the edges of western history, living through freedom and post-colonialism and exile, all in half a lifetime. Born into the sureness of a caste, religion, or even a tribe, deserting it, they must find equivalents in the post-industrial state.

I have lived my intellectual life among such speeded-up people, shape-changers, scholars, and artists with thousand-year lifespans. I have learned to mimic their anxieties, to see my world through their eyes, but I can only envy the luridness of their visions, the transformations wrought by a Rushdie or Mukherjee. The closest I ever came was in the tracing of Kentucky counties, painted and pasted and patiently memorized. I have colored my life within in the borders. I'm the framework between the bins.

II

THE

LATIN

QUARTER

IN ONE OF THE MOST UNUSUAL NOVELS of this century, Juan Rulfo's *Pedro Páramo* (1959), the unnamed narrator goes to a village in search of his father. Its first sentence announces: "I came to Comala because I was told that my father, a certain Pedro Páramo, was living there." It's just a little book, 123 pages in the standard Lysander Kemp translation.

Alternately, I could say: *I came to Lac-Mégantic, Québec, because it is the place my father, a certain Léo Joseph Pierre Roméo Blais, known to me as Lee R. Blaise, came from.*

The father, Rulfo's narrator learns, is dead. Comala is dead, a densely populated ghost town of rumors, passions, and vendettas, and soon the searcher will die—he's the only dead, first-person narrator I know of—but the search goes on. The dead are linked with the living and with each other and frequently ask, "Are you dead or alive? I forget." Death is not the end point. The erasure of a single life does not affect the community. Continuity, survival, *survivance,* is the point.

Mexico and Canada: what could be more different? But Lac-Mégantic is a Catholic, French-Canadian village culture, it is contiguous with Latin America, as though the Protestant, individualist bulk of the United States never existed. It *is* Latin America.

The Pluto in my Calvinist orbit is Latin America.

"Make him pay for the way he forgot us," his mother begs the narrator. But fathers never pay. It's always the wife and sons. All men are unfaithful, all men abandon their families. It's the cult of machismo. The book suggests that the search for a father, particularly an unknown father, signals the return to origins and a surrender to death. The compulsion to learn the truth of one's origins and to make peace with one's father is stronger than survival itself. We make this journey back to the headwaters like spawning salmon, turning grotesque in our single-mindedness.

This book, not Rulfo's, is about me and my father, and it's about that dark planet I've called Québec, but it is also about a darker planet called aging and death, and masculinity or maybe just plain old-fashioned identity. I have never inhabited those planets confidently. There is a gap between the "me" who has lived through certain experiences, who travels the world constantly with a responsible position, who has married only once and fathered two grown sons, who generally behaves correctly, and the "me" who comes from nowhere and has no fixed identity, and who could be a visitor from another solar system.

Ever since a breakdown that corresponded to the breakup of my parents' marriage when I was a junior in college, a geology major, my world has split in two, and the only bridge between those halves has been books. I have trusted books to read my mind, even to stand, like *Pedro Páramo,* as surrogate autobiographies.

In the winter of 1960, the Christmas break, I was reading as much for visual as verbal satisfaction, working my way through the rainbow of Scribner's paperbacks with their color-coded spines (green for Fitzgerald, blue for Hemingway, yellows and reds and purples whose designations I now forget). In the dull Pittsburgh winter that my parents separated, I had a paintpot of color at my feet. I was There and not-There, a migratory bird. The night that my father attacked my mother, tearing up the contract of their marriage by breaking her nose and blackening both eyes, I was sprawled on a half-sofa in an upstairs room, reading. That was the nature of my breakdown: I suddenly couldn't go on with my college life, my geology studies, my labs, my fraternity, all the social futilities. I couldn't even get off the couch. She came to the door, a few minutes after the garage door slammed and said, "I must have walked into something."

Life without my parents' unspoken, unacted erotic violence is literally unimaginable to me—that is, not available to my imagination—which guarantees I'll always be a son and not a husband or a father in everything I write. Life after their divorce seems lacking in pain and moral authority. In order to imagine stories, I need the shelter of their marriage, their complications and polarities. Within their marriage, within the world of my growing-up, all things are possible.

For over a year, my world had been pulling away from me. My parents were divorcing. My father was transformed: indifferent to the store, leaving it locked unless my mother or I opened up. He was out every night with his other woman, denying it if confronted, returning home only at three in the morning, drunk, to pick up shirts and suits. We avoided him. Whenever he entered, I gripped my book all the harder, rather than intervene. If we're lucky, we may see the rise of passions in our children, but the grown child never expects to see it in his aging parents. My mother had lost her confidence. My father was on the warpath.

It was a bloody colonial uprising.

I PLAY ALL SPORTS as badly as they can be played; I exercise vigorously enough to be a rock (or a waif), but given my "dystrophy" the exercising has little cosmetic effect, except for a reptilian pulse-rate. And I feel at times my body, in its strain to know grace and strength and a kind of quiet pride, rather than shame and awkwardness, is a template of similar gaps in my understanding of the world and my behavior in it.

When I was younger, just beginning my adolescent growth, I wondered how tall I would get. Dramatic growth seemed the only way out of a permanent shiny-pants, sportcoat-wearing adolescence. My mother was tall, at five-nine. My father was, in absolute terms, a short man, at five-seven. But within his family of under five-footers, he was considered a giant. Therefore, I tried to reason, did I inherit one gene for shortness, one for tall—or a double gene for height? Is the world quantitative, or qualitative? (I ended up at five-eleven and a half.) My mother had education and trained skills; my father had none. She clearly was an intelligent woman, but how to separate her intelligence from her training? My father eluded all measures of intelligence; he might have been a brute or, given his successful functioning in a world so alien to his talents, a genius. I throw right-handed, but do everything else left-handed. Am I right-handed or left-handed? I walk slowly and I run slowly. But since I run every day shouldn't frequent running at least improve my walking speed? Taken to their limits, these are identity questions. If every category is discrete, how do we reach a synthesis, an identity?

Until I started high school in Pittsburgh, I was accustomed to being, far and away, the smartest boy in any school—I mean the smartest *by factors*. Is that a measure of me, of childhood, of adolescence, of Pittsburgh, or of rural southern schools? (Every child on this planet is a genius in his first two years, processing language and mastering motor skills.) I had a genius of a childhood and then something happened.

In the Pittsburgh suburbs, I was in my mother's world of trained intellects with professional ambitions. I was good, sort of high-mediocre, but I trailed the best minds *by factors*.

In my childhood Florida, I was in my father's world, something elemental, where training didn't help. He was functionally literate, but it was rage and charm that took the place of language.

He got by in our Pittsburgh store by having my high school friends conduct the inventories, by having me or my mother write up the orders, and by his own ability to add and memorize numbers. He could add up columns of figures in his head, lips making those French noises, as fast as I could enter them on the old adding machine. Since the retail furniture markup was 43 percent over cost, he could calculate the retail price on any cost without consulting the plastic wheel that most buyers carry with them like lifesaving medication. (I carried the wheel, hoping always to catch him in a mistake.) Nothing related to furniture required the slightest effort of retention on his part (just like me with geography, or the names of birds and fish and animals, and eventually long lists of kings and popes and emperors); model numbers, upholstery numbers, telephone numbers, and addresses. My mother wrote the checks, filled in the loan forms. When he wrote, he held the pen so tightly it tore the paper, shredded the carbons, scarred the desktop underneath. He wrote "Phg" for Pittsburgh, to the confusion of shippers, despite my efforts to change him. He never read a paper, he knew nothing of events going on except for the heartbreaking Pirates and Steelers, two last-place finishers in the decade of the '50s.

What sort of man am I describing? I think my mother was high-mediocre. I think my father was touched with genius. And his tragedy is that he never knew it, and no one ever told him.

I retained a shell of that original genius, enough to function in the artistic world. But if I'm diminished from what I was, it isn't simply a matter of age or of adjusting to stiffer, suburban competition. It was a change of worlds.

ENGRAVED OVER THE LIBRARY STEPS of my alma mater, Denison University, are the lines from Thoreau: "Books are the treasured wealth of the world, the fit inheritance of generations and nations." I remember one day in my senior year, after I'd come back to school and had changed my major from geology to English and my am-

bition from paleontology to writing, sitting down and
staring at the inscription as though it held my future. That's
a troublesome phrase: *Books are the inheritance.* Inheritance
means both that which has been received and that which
is still to come. I'd just been disinherited by my father who
had remarried and gone to Mexico. So far as I knew, I had
no future beyond that semester on government loan.

My mother had moved into a boardinghouse and
taken a lamp-selling job downtown. The house was sold
(the land alone, in ultra-suburban Upper St. Clair is now
worth tens of thousands. The house, I should think, a good
quarter-million. My father's financial instincts, as always,
were sound. It's his character that let him down). The
stores were sold and everything auctioned off. My mother's "50–50 share," as determined by a shady accountant
who was one of my father's weekend "fishing" friends,
came to twelve thousand dollars because she chose not to
challenge a line of the agreement. (When she died in Canada
twenty-five years later, after a dozen years in a nursing
home, the original nest egg, through secure investments,
had grown to eighteen thousand. She hadn't touched a
penny.)

I had dropped out of school shortly after the attack
on my mother. I'd picked up a book—it happened to be
The Red and the Black—and that started me on a promise:
I would read a book a day, and I kept that promise during
a semester of breakdown and a busboy's job in Ft. Lauderdale, then as a Freedom Rider in Tennessee, and a summer school waiter and student at Northwestern, then back
at Denison for a senior year, then the summer at Harvard
with Malamud, and a year of working in a Boston book-

store, and then two years of graduate school, and the next three years, until I got to Canada. Those thousands of books, unassigned and unlectured upon, read without guidance or credit or commentary, linked in no real chain except rumor, chance encounter, a rave notice, random praise, are my education.

The inheritance turned out to be a prophecy. The invisible world of permanent forms was speaking to me. A few years later, I would encounter, in Sartre's *Saint Genet,* lines that I took so personally that I memorized them and made them the epigraph to my first book (still about a dozen years away): "Indeed, it is not unusual for the memory to condense into a single mythic moment the contingencies and perpetual rebeginnings of an individual human history." In other words, memory is a guide to the future as well as a recollection of the past. Not only that, but memory promises *re*-beginnings, second acts. Memory condenses the time-flow, past and future. Time flows both ways. Linearity is an illusion. Memory is the antidote to the pernicious nihilism of the Eveready pink rabbit.

Books did my living for me. I have converted my favorite novels into autobiographies; *Pedro Páramo* is one of those books, like Céline's *Death on the Installment Plan* ("Mort à Crédit"), *The Sentimental Education,* or much of Faulkner. They entered my life at a time when I was searching for models of my own experience. When, in essence, my experience had betrayed me. The South was too far away. Canada was in my future. The American present was a kind of pestilence. Books shaped my experiences for me.

Céline helped me understand, and even grow fond of, the sheer mendacity of the furniture-trade, the various lowlifes and mafiosi and indictable scoundrels who'd inhabited my growing-up, and the mixture of terror, reverence, and contempt that I perceived in my father's attitude to the business world. The lingering aftereffect of that book was so great that in 1968 I tramped through the *passages* of Paris taking pictures of the hagglers' stalls under the glass arcades. It was a perfect, apocalyptic time to be doing it, the close of an era, since my wife and I were prisoners of the events of 1968—unable to get out of Paris as students burned barricades in the streets, Robert Kennedy was assassinated, and de Gaulle lectured the nation on committing *"chie-en-lit."*

And the revered Faulkner, much earlier, had surrounded me with a forest of language, with archetypes of character, and with a socio-historical pessimism that I knew to be true from my own childhood. I'd been exposed to an inland, north-Florida empire of social reaction—call it damnation—and of natural beauty—call it ferocity—and of chiseled character-types—call them Crackers—whose features, accents, language, are burned into my memory even today.

Pedro Páramo is a book of my life because it links an apparently hallucinated, apparently surreal world with one that I have since learned is absolutely true, factual, even unremarkable. If for no other reason than the following sentences, I would treasure *Pedro Páramo:* "At daybreak the day gives a turn, slowly. You can almost hear the rusty hinges of the world. The vibration of this ancient world as it tilts the darkness off itself." The death, in other words, of an older, harsher world. And it is because of Juan Rulfo that I can say without exaggeration or straining for effect:

"My aunt died four times the year of her five births."

That is the ancient world my father was born to and lived through.

All my life I've been looking for points of entry into an earlier world, in India, the South, Montréal. I memorized my mother's 1920s British atlas when I was a small child (I still remember its mildewed Florida smell, the mold stains on its cover page). In her world (hence, in mine) every continent but Europe still had its unexplored territories, air-brushed voids without mountains or political divisions where rivers stopped. The officially unexplored became the unintended focus of all my attention. It was a post-modern, Edwardian atlas. When an authoritative map suddenly ends and admits defeat, it renders all information suspect. It elevates the wildest speculation to possible truth.

I used to spend hours with her father's pocket-sized (thick but narrow) Canadian bird-watchers' guide. There were paintings of passenger pigeons and ivory-billed woodpeckers in that guide, and the maps of the United States that showed fuzzy patches in the southwest labeled only "Indian Territories." She and I sat on the bed in our shanty in the woods near Tavares, Florida, and identified the smears of bright color, the winter songbirds like painted buntings and scarlet tanagers, just inches away on the other side of the screen. Like Darwin on the Galápagos, I could press against the screen and they would hop unafraid up to the window, picking food off the ledge. These birds coexisted with extinct species, with Indian territories. I searched the skies for pterodactyls.

What *Pedro Páramo* suggests to me now is that in seek-

ing knowledge of my father I am plunging into an undertow. Learning one's father's passions and his crimes is
the essence of all forbidden knowledge. Reentering the skin
of the father is the source of the Oedipus complex. And
the horror of it is probably the inspiration for Dracula,
Frankenstein, the Thing, and the Bodysnatchers. My father
is gone; what I do not know of him now is what I do not
know in myself. What I discover is only what I can finally
admit. And part of me says I welcome the undertow, I
want to know, I want to be swept away.

Good books read us, in our needs, more than we read
them. Pedro Páramo is my father too, French-Canadians
are as Latin American as Mexicans. My father's life begins
to make sense to me if I see Lac-Mégantic as a placid
Tijuana or Nogales and the American border of Maine and
New Hampshire as the same bug-zapper—an annihilating
lure—south-Texas and Arizona are to Mexicans and central Americans. It has helped me see my father's boxing
and boozing and marriages; his harmonica playing, tap
dancing, and crooning charm; his women and his police
record as discards in his gringo-izing. By the time I knew
him, the outer transformation was nearly complete.

CHAPTER   EIGHT

THINK OF THIS as an old photo, sepia-toned, drab but precise. It is a hot summer day, June 22, 1888. A northern summer light etches the leaves, the woodgrains, the homespun threads and the brown septic water in the standing puddles. My father will not be born for another seventeen years, but his parents, Achille and Orienne, have been married six years and have already buried two of their five children and before the summer is over they will bury the other three. My grandmother of course is pregnant.

One can only imagine the flies, the airborne stench from so much uncleared human and animal waste, the mosquitoes and disease from acres of standing water. Only the pulp company, which runs twenty-four hours a day, has electricity. There is no running water, no civic hygiene. Everything is wooden—the sidewalks, the houses, the hotels, and the boards over the open sewers and mud. Mud is still the glue of civilization, brick-builder and filler of cracks. Not yet the enemy of all progress. With mud and lumber, hammer and nails, every man is a king.

Mégantic could be in a Flemish landscape painting, a single deep horizon of children and animals, haylofts and drunkards, priests and adventurers, all lounging in the sun, some snoring, some whittling, others plotting fornication. On the fringes of town, men hunt and fish, women wash and hike their skirts, kids pull down the *bécosses,* exposing old men pulling their carrots, or stare through the wooden slats at girls cleaning themselves with catalog pages. Ladies keep hankies over their noses. Men duck into the bars. The stench of stale beer is preferable to the sidewalk and backyard odors. Norman Rockwell *à la belle province.* This is the life and the language of rural French peasants of the 17th century.

Ste-Agnès Church and the Sacré-Cœur Monastery dominate the village. Father Cousineau, a bulky, square-jawed priest with dark, thinning hair in the Karl Malden tradition rushes by, ledger book in hand, on his way to another funeral or christening. Sometimes, it's rumored, he forgets which one and is halfway through the service before correcting himself.

Something special, this day, is in the air. Crowds have gathered in front of Mayor McAuley's Hotel. Down the wooden sidewalk strides a privately appointed deputy sheriff, Lucius Warren, holding an arrest-warrant for Donald Morrison, known to be drinking as usual at his favorite bar. It is not inconceivable that my grandfather, Achille Blais, one of a group of young French millworkers, is on the sidewalk. Most of the crowd is Scots. Normally they'd push and taunt, keeping each other from their favorite bars. Not today.

Donald Morrison is more a Hollywood hero than Canadian. Sullen, ignorant, drunken, powerful, a returned cowboy, a loner. Canadians prefer their heroes sociable, progressive, law-enforcing, above local and ethnic passions. In Canadian books, schoolteachers and politicians and Mounties are heroes; Americans prefer rebellious schoolkids, outlaws, and private eyes. Donald Morrison will break the law today to protect his property, to avenge his father, to resist a loan shark. There's something lonely and tragic about Donald Morrison.

He had been a cowboy out in Manitoba. He'd returned from the west, a witness to the French and Indian (*métis*) raids against white settlers, only to find his old Québec home devastated, his patrimony sold, his father humiliated and in debt, and the goddamned French moving in. Hell, it's worse than Manitoba! It's *Gone with the Wind* without the beautiful ladies and wisteria, without the white columns and masked balls. But there's a fire, by god. And vengeance.

The bloodsucking moneylender is the mayor, sawmill manager and hotelier, Malcolm McAuley. He feeds, they like to say, on his own kind, the trusting, Isle of Lewis-born, Gaelic-speaking Scots. McAuley is into Murdo Morrison, Donald's 70-year-old father, for $1100 at 9 percent interest. The trouble is, McAuley held back four hundred dollars of the principal as security, while charging interest on the full amount. At foreclosure he'd sold Murdo's farm to a French-Canadian family, the Duquettes, for $1500. And the farm had mysteriously burned down.

That's an arson charge in Lucius Warren's hand.

Rough, vagrant, but loyal to his father, Donald Morrison is everything the sleek hound McAuley is not. It is McAuley who hired the sleazy Warren, otherwise known as a whiskey-runner to the Canadian railway workers putting a CPR line through dry Maine, to do his dirty work. Morrison obliges Warren by coming out of the bar on command, then shoots him in front of a crowd in broad daylight.

He flees and enters local myth and, briefly, the national headlines as "The Megantic Outlaw."

There are enough compelling stories here for a miniseries. We have a tale of crime and punishment, of loyalty and betrayal, a lone, uncomplicated man pushed to uncharacteristic honor, a powerful man of no scruples, a colorful East Coast frontier, quaint ethnic divisions, mass death on a plague-like scale, a subculture of bordertown smugglers, a churchly authority, a murder, asylum, and a chase. On top of it we have an historical era and an entire people and culture, the highland Scots, drawing to a close ("you can almost hear the rusty hinge of the world . . . "), and a tentative national authority trying to exercise its legal and civil powers over an alien people. Márquez should be so blessed!

I'll even throw in my grandfather, Achille, as an ironic narrator.

During the fall and winter the old Scottish crofters hide and feed young Morrison, and the Caledonian Society raises money for his defense while the Mounties comb the hillsides. The mayor's power is broken, and American interests take over the mills. In the spring of 1889, Morrison is wounded and captured, but his trial in Montréal results in a manslaughter conviction, not murder. Though he sickens and dies in prison, he nearly beats the rap.

There's something Faulknerian in all this. Families like mine, Snopeses from the original Frenchman's Bend, are moving in and taking over despite their mortality rates.

The Celtic gods are in retreat, the wild ways of the high-landers will soon disappear, leaving only the quaint place-names, the Sherbrookes and Stansteads, in French-dominated eastern Québec.

The lumber companies demand and get—over the editorial objection of *Le Travailleur* (the town's newspaper)—permission to flood the fields with standing water. Thirteen of the eighteen children of Achille and Orienne Blais die before the age of five. The first physical failing is likely to be their last: appendix, heart, diabetes, stroke, cancer, not to mention the myriad assaults on the glands, the infections, the communal diseases. The wonder is survival, not death. How do the survivors even process their good fortune—luck, entitlement, grace? Survival is guilt and a license to plunder. All the survivors—Corinne, Lena, Bella, Oliva, and Léo—were born after the installation of running water and the passing of civic hygiene codes. Corinne will die in her twenties, in Manchester.

Meanwhile, the whiskey-fed railway workers push the CPR tracks across Maine to link Halifax with Montréal and the West. Immigrants get off the train after their sealed transit across Maine, scratch at lice, and cough their lungs out on their two-hour recoaling stop. The town turns out every day to gawk at this ungodly effluvia in their black hats and beards, women in shawls wearing all their jewelry. It's the great age of European immigration to North America. Russians, Poles, Italians, Slovaks, Ukrainians, Ruthenians, and Magyars, all passing through a French-Canadian village on their way to Montréal and land out west. Shades of Macondo and Márquez's gypsies in *One Hundred Years of Solitude*. Mégantic as Ellis Island. Gypsies, tramps, and thieves. Typhoid, diphtheria, scarlet fever, tuberculosis, smallpox, dysentery.

FIVE YEARS BEFORE the mildly upbeat tale of Donald Morrison, out in the real Canadian west of Manitoba, the Mounties had put a dramatic end to the "Riel Rebellion," the struggle led by the young Métis (mixed-blood French and Cree) leader, Louis Riel, who was intent on stopping the incorporation of Manitoba into Canada and establishing an Indian and Métis homeland. Riel was hunted down, hanged, and vilified for most of a century. Like Benedict Arnold, like my father, like me, Riel was a border-hopper of suspect loyalty. The Canadian traitor-patriot was a naturalized American citizen, even a Republican.

The lesson of history appears to be if you're going to take up arms against the Sergeant Prestons of Canada, it helps to be white and English-speaking, with the Caledonian Society lawyers behind you. Forty-odd years ago when I was a schoolboy in Winnipeg in the heart of Riel's lost Métis empire, I studied him as a traitor, his name as cursed as Abraham Lincoln's had been in Florida a few months earlier. These days, thanks to the rise of a *québécois* consciousness, Louis Riel is recognized as a problematic Canadian hero, a people's leader, a resister. Now schools are named for him, books are written, and a TV miniseries gained a huge national audience.

Less than a decade after the hanging of Riel in 1885, my mother's people began arriving in the sanitized western sections of Manitoba and eastern Saskatchewan. My grandfather started his medical practice, married, bred his horses, and imported strains of Asian fruit trees to grow on the Prairies. From his village of Wawanesa, smaller and less cosmopolitan than Mégantic at the same time, he bred horses and fruit trees and later built the country's largest insurance company. Six of their ten children reached adulthood, all but one went to college, and their youngest is less than twenty years older than I. My father's oldest siblings were born well over a century ago. My parents were nearly the same age, but the oldest and youngest of different generations, looking out on different centuries.

IN THE EPIC SWEEP of Canada just one hundred years ago, it is possible that Donald Morrison saw Louis Riel, or that one or two of those immigrants who stretched their legs in the train station of Mégantic, or perhaps raised their heads from shawls or fur hats and looked into the incredulous eyes of Achille Blais, found themselves six months or a year later being attended to on the Prairies by my other grandfather, the Manitoba doctor.

It amazes me to think I'm the grandson of sharecroppers and homesteaders. The son of an expatriate-Canadian Prague designer and a boxer.

CHAPTER NINE

IT'S A QUIET SUMMER DAY in Montréal in 1989 in the McGill University Library and I'm scrolling through time, or more precisely, through the *New York Times* microfilms. For the past three days I've been attending a conference at Laval University in Quebec City on *la francophonie américaine*, the influence of Québec on New England's "Franco" population. I'd given a paper, and I'd met the professional researchers in my temporary and adopted field, serious people with names like mine from Maine and New England, and even one from Paris. In fact, that's what I'm doing in the McGill microfilm room— tracing the footnotes in François Weil's book, *Les Franco-Américains* (Tours, 1989), back to their sources. The best book on Franco-Americans, not surprisingly, is by a Parisian Jew from the École Normale Supérieure, unattached to the cause and using foreign methods of historical research.

Weil's book alludes to the anti-French backlash in New England and cites, but does not quote, two front-page *New York Times* editorials against French-Canadian immigration. The text of those long-dead editorials now glows before me on the screen. It's shocking to read such blatant racism—xenophobic, nativist, bigoted—but it's also hard to concentrate on the central text with all the sidebars of killings, corruption, and anonymous cruelties pushing in from the margins. The *Ragtime* spirit takes over. Fiction, as always, competes with history.

Reading old papers is like the dozens of times I've packed the china, balling up wads of newspaper to use as protection. And at the other end, sometimes years later, smoothing out the balls of paper and reading them with new fascination, new meaning. All those comic strips, those box-scores, those scandals, those supermarket ads with cheaper prices and defunct products live again. Or, one might say, live free from their original context and establish a new reality. Junk becomes a voice from the grave. Every wiggle of the Zeitgeist is freshly significant. The monolith of the quotidian breaks down into the peculiar poignance of a discontinuous present. Post-modernist paper-waddings.

On the 4th of July, an immigrant family in the South Bronx climbs up to their rooftop to watch the fireworks display in their adopted country. On a neighboring rooftop, random, drunken, celebratory gunfire erupts in syncopation with the fireworks and the immigrants' four-year-old daughter falls dead. South Bronx, gunfire: of course, we say, so what? But the immigrants are German, the girl is named Hildegarde and this is the 4th of July, 1889, exactly a hundred years ago. *Plus ça change.*

Hildegarde's senseless death impinging upon (and momentarily erasing) the *Times* editorial is the process of autobiography in a single image. The principle of priority is elusive and threatens at any moment to disintegrate. The main story is usurped by propinquity, by sheer tragic anonymity.

Can it be that the universe remains random, but that nothing in a single human life is coincidental? Any shred of memory that survives, no matter how insignificant, becomes a focus. Any piece of junk from my father, after two marriages carried it off, is a kind of moon rock: common as dirt, but invaluable. Any shred of my father that survives clones him briefly into the protector and destroyer of my life. And, I begin to think, he can still guide me. As in *Pedro Páramo,* a dead man shall lead me.

One hundred years ago, when French-Canadians were pouring (the *Times* prefers "swarming") into New England to soak up the pulp and textile and shoemaking jobs in Manchester, Lowell, Chicopee, Fall River, Lewiston, Pawtucket, and Woonsocket, the organized "responsible" opinion of America was arrayed against them as viciously as anything faced by present-day Chicanos. Quebeckers from ten miles over the border were as exotic as Samoans. Their mysterious loyalty to church and language and family, tight as plaque to a molar, was cited as an untransferable, unassimilatable, conspiratorial threat to the American way of life.

These are the words of the *New York Times,* July 5, 1889:

> The French-Canadians do not form a very conspicuous element in the population of this city or of this State, although it is rather startling to be informed that some 25,000 of them are living and working in Clinton County. In those New England States which adjoin Lower Canada the influx of French-Canadians is much more interesting

and important. The immigrants, tempted by a more genial climate than their own and a higher rate of wages, have swarmed into the factories and taken up the farms abandoned by the natives as unprofitable. They are so much more prolific than their neighbors that the proportion of them to the whole community, whenever they have established themselves, tends to increase with surprising rapidity.

Whether this immigration is a good thing or a bad thing for the country is a question the answer to which depends upon the same considerations that determine the character of any other immigration. It may be summed up in the general statement that immigration is a source of strength to the country insofar as it is capable of being readily assimilated and Americanized. It is not only, in some cases it is not mainly, our English-speaking immigrants who fulfill this condition best. Of course a foreigner who arrives in this country at a mature age entirely ignorant of its language and its customs, can become but a very imperfect American. But if he means to become an American, his children may be good citizens as if their ancestors for generations had been born upon our soil. They are sources of strength to the Republic, not only economically, but politically and socially.

Tried by this standard, it must be owned that the French-Canadians do not give promise of incorporating themselves with our body politic.

Their convention, held on Tuesday in this city, contemplates united action on all questions that may arise from their residence in the U.S. The united action of one element of our population in behalf of its own special opinions and customs is, as to the rest of the community, a separate action. It indicates that those who take it mean to remain a foreign body, and such a body, under a form of government and with a structure of society like ours, is a source of political and social weakness. The advantages that we derive from the sojourn in this country of the Chinese, for example, are purely economic. The fact that they remain and thrive is conclusive proof that they are needed and useful, and that they do work which would be done worse or more dearly if they were not here. But their usefulness ends here, and our interests require something more. We need that our immigrants should be not only good workmen, but good citizens. The French-Canadians mean to retain in this country, as for two centuries they have succeeded in retaining in Canada, the religion and language of their ancestors, as distinctive badges of their separation from their neighbors. Comparatively few of them become citizens at all, and those who do rate their citizenship so low and understand its duties so little that the power of voting renders them much less acceptable members of the community than they would be without it.

Of course all this does not furnish any reason

whatever for persecuting the French-Canadians who are already among us or even for taking measures to reduce the volume of immigration from this source. They will become dangerous only in case they become numerous enough and adopt the practice of naturalization extensively enough to hold the balance of power in American communities. In that case there would be a real danger that they might demand and obtain legislation favorable to their special and separate interests, and in the same degree hostile to the general interests of the community. The danger has scarcely yet become imminent in any American community, but it is foreshadowed distinctly enough to make it a patriotic duty for all Americans, in which the French-Canadian population is considerable, to insist upon maintaining American political principles against all assaults.

The French-Canadians, in signaling their intention to export the protections (like the church and the St-Jean-Baptiste Society) that had buttressed their survival for three hundred years in Canada, were one of the first immigrant people in the United States to challenge the myth of the Melting Pot. That is, the first to raise contemporary issues of multiculturalism. They were coming for economic reasons and had no intention of surrendering their language or religion. They were the first whites to come to the United States with Third World values. They were, as a leading separatist theorizer, Pierre Vallières, was to call them seventy-five years later, *les nègres blancs d'Amérique,* the so-called "white niggers of America." There's a famous Québec poem, a rallying cry of Québec separatists of my generation, *Parlez-blanc* (Speak White).

I knew the usual Anglo designations for the French— Pepsis, Peppers—but I'd seriously doubted the importation of a British or an American vocabulary. "Speak White" struck me as histrionic, a yearning for provocation.

ONE OF THE SHOCKING MOMENTS in my life came on Prince Edward Island in the early 1970s, in a consciously maintained *Anne of Green Gables*-style tourist home. My wife and I and the children had checked in for one comfortable night after the long drive from Montréal, in preparation for two weeks of camping out. I with a French name and Québec plates; my wife with a foreign name and dark skin. The old Scottish-Canadian lady, pouring tea to the guests as we watched the evening news, with its usual bulletins from Québec, announced her frustration: "I just can't understand it. White people built this country and the niggers are trying to tear it apart."

IT WAS RACISM that ended our life in Canada in the late 1970s. We'd moved to Toronto in 1978—Toronto the Good, Toronto the culmination of an English-Canadian writer's dream of access and power. We were unprepared for the virulence of anti-Indian ("Paki-bashing") sentiment in Toronto, the daily insults Bharati faced. By 1980 we'd resigned our jobs and emigrated to the States to start new lives at the age of forty. With my American faith in rebeginnings, I was confident, and I paid a heavy price. With my wife's Hindu fatalism, she was not, and the fates have been considerably kinder.

I would like to be one for whom crowds turn out; I have become one who turns out crowds. Between 1982 and 1987, we couldn't afford milk and orange juice at the same breakfast. From 1987 till 1990, I held four jobs a year in New York, each paying five thousand dollars; my wife held two, and taught six classes a semester. The rise in our fortunes these past two years has been steep.

THE TIMES DISMISSED the Chinese as "sojourners," barred from citizenship on racial grounds, while acknowledging the contribution of their useful labor at coolie wages. French-Canadians were likened to Chinese in their sheer alienness, but represented a far greater danger to the United States because, as whites, they were eligible for citizenship. The immigrant waves from eastern and southern Europe, despite their greater linguistic and religious differences from mainstream America, were somehow proving themselves more assimilable, in the eyes of the *Times,* than the French-Canadians, though one cannot imagine them working for more than coolie wages in their downtown and Brooklyn sweatshops or restricting their birthrates in the interest of preserving Anglo-Saxon domination.

One group depresses the standard of living; other groups working for even less perform a valuable service—provided we never admit them to citizenship. Damned for their passivity to the Roman Catholic Church and damned for their aggressiveness in snapping up derelict farms and low-end jobs. Damned if they chose naturalization—the quicker to absorb us—or damned if they scorned it—too proud of their differences. To the *Times,* the French-Canadians were zombies with a high sperm count, body-snatchers who were now among us and admissible for citizenship if we didn't wake up in time.

Behind the appeal to traditional assimilist assumptions lurked unstated fears. French-Canadians, like today's Latin Americans, were an army poised at the border ready to march into the country. No ships to turn back, no Ellis Island to detain them, no effective way of turning off the tap. And worse, the French-Canadians, like other undesirables, were sexual guerrillas. They could replenish their numbers lost to mortality and emigration with rodent-like rapidity. (In Québec, survival of the race had always demanded an explicitly sexual strategy, the *revanche des berceaux,* or "revenge of the cradles.") The other notoriously fecund races, the Chinese and Indians, were legally barred from America. Hatred of the French-Canadian was a sexual terror, a racist, white-nigger terror. Even my mother, enlightened in most matters, feared Catholic hospitals, knowing that the doctors and nurses were under secret orders from the Pope to kill Protestant mothers if a Catholic baby was threatened.

I think of my father's family, the middle-aged parents and their five surviving children arriving in Manchester in 1913, and of my eight-year-old father, a bright, observant boy, put to work for twenty-five cents a day at Amoskeag Mills. These are the people the *Times* is writing against. I read the Yankee foreman's assessments of my grandparents (good workers, responsible) and of my Uncle Oliva (trouble, drunk, fights, and finally just "French" who finally walked out the door and actually stayed in France), and I feel a kind of class rage, almost a racial resentment, rising. I think of Sondheim's *Sweeney Todd* and I want to sing for my father: "He saw how decent men behave/and he never forgot/and he never forgave."

The *New York Times* hadn't yet finished with the French-Canadian peril. Just a hundred years ago, June 6, 1892, they published a second editorial. This time, they had done their scholarly duty: they had heavy-duty names, like Francis Parkman, to back up their prejudice:

It is said there are more French-Canadians in New-England than there are in Canada. There are 400,000 in round numbers in New-England at this time, and in five of its principal cities they have the balance of power to-day. The Irish-American population is still larger, and it probably had the balance of power in more places, but to-day the second and third generations of the Irish-Americans are so nearly assimilated to the native population in political and social life that neither their religion nor its adjunct, the parochial school, is able to keep them out of the strong currents of American life. With the French-Canadian this is not the case. *Mr. Francis Parkman* has ably pointed out their singular tenacity as a race and their extreme devotion to their religion, and their transplantations to the manufacturing centers and the rural districts in New-England mean that Quebec is transferred bodily to Manchester and Fall River and Lowell. Not only does the French *curé* follow the French peasantry to their new homes, but he takes with him the parish church, the ample clerical residence, the convent for the sisters, and the parochial school for the education of the children. He also perpetuates the French ideas and aspirations through the French language, and places all the obstacles possible in the way of the assimilation of these people to our American life and thought. There is something still more imperfect in this transplantation. These people are in New-England as an organized body, whose motto is *Notre religion, notre langue, et nos mœurs.* This body is ruled by a principle directly opposite to that which has made New-England what it is. It depresses to the lowest point possible the idea of personal responsibility and limits the freedom which it permits.

It is next to impossible to penetrate this mass of protected and secluded humanity with modern ideas or to induce them to interest themselves in democratic institutions and methods of government. They are almost as much out of reach as if they were living in a remote part of the Province of Quebec. No other people, except the Indians, are so persistent in repeating themselves. Where they halt they stay, and where they stay, they multiply and cover the earth. *Dr. Egbert C. Smyth,* in a paper just published by the American Antiquarian Society, has been at great pains to trace intelligently the extent of this immigration, and in his opinion the migration of these people is part of a priestly scheme now fervently fostered in Canada for the purpose of bringing New-England under the control of the Roman Catholic faith. He points out that this is the avowed purpose of the secret society to which every adult French-Canadian belongs, and that the prayers and the earnest effort of these people are to turn the tables in New-England by the aid of the silent forces which they control.

What will the New Englanders do about it? There is apparently but one way in which this conquest can be arrested. That is to compel the use of the English language in all the schools by American citizens. This is the point which *Archbishop Ireland,* with his intense American feelings, has had in view in the Faribault experiment in Minnesota. In that state all the European languages are constantly spoken by people who live in sections, and the placing of their children in the public instead of the parochial schools means that the children will become loyal and intelligent American citizens. One of the chief reasons why his scheme appeals strongly to Americans is that it is likely to be more effective than anything else in destroying the race prejudice and divisions in the Nation. It is through their parochial schools, in which French is exclusively used, that the French-Canadians in New-England are able to keep themselves from any sympathetic or intelligent contact with our American political and social life, and apparently the only way in which the danger which threatens New-England traditions can be averted is by national legislation which shall compel the use of English language in all schools, public and private, throughout the Nation. It has been hoped heretofore that the free pressure of American life upon our foreign populations was sufficient to change all new-comers, no matter what might have been their previous affiliations, into interested and enthusiastic Americans in the course of one or two generations, but when an immigration like that of the French-Canadians in New-England takes possession of the centers of population and has the power to crowd out the less productive race in the struggle for the survival of the fittest, the free action of American institutions is not strong enough to counteract these designs, and it is only by national legislation that the difficulty can be reached. It seems like an idle alarm to sound the note of danger at this early day in New-England, but the way in which thoughtful people in the New-England states are now gathering statistics and evidence as to the nature and extent of the problem which confronts them is indicative of great uneasiness.

Everything's relative, of course. A friend told me of his first encounter with the French. He was fresh from Brooklyn, teaching at Brown, and living in a second-floor apartment in densely French Woonsocket. He woke up one morning to a man's shouting under his window, "Turn on the Jew!" Then, "Turn off the Jew!" Panicked, his worst fears confirmed, he ran to his window. The fat little janitor kept repeating the order. The lights dimmed, then brightened, on his command. "Jew's back," he shouted up. Though it's been nearly forty years, and my friend solved the "Jew–jus–juice" confusion immediately, deep down, there'll always be that little shadow of doubt.

CHAPTER TEN

A HUNDRED YEARS after that *Times* editorial, in the summer of 1989, I went to Lac-Mégantic for the first time because it was the place my father came from. My grandparents, Mémère and Pépère, died before I was born. Despite the fact that I was never a French-Canadian, never spoke the language as a child, never took a puck in the face for old Québec, never was a Catholic, never munched my way through a proper New Year's Day *réveillon,* and never dug a drunken uncle from under a pile of January overcoats, Québec is in a profound sense my home. "Profound" in its French sense, *profond,* meaning deep.

In the Bengali language and culture, the father's birthplace is one's *desh,* the operative social determinant in any child's life, hence his only real home. It is possible to have a home yet never to have seen it—my wife has never visited her *desh* of Faridpur, now a village in Bangladesh less than two hundred miles from Calcutta—approximately Lac-Mégantic's distance from Boston.

Desh means home, in the German sense of *Heimat,* in the French of *patrie.* It is a political and cultural and psychological concept, it has mystical and dangerous *volkisch* elements in it. "Amar sonar bangladesh" rhapsodized the greatest Bengali of them all, Rabindranath Tagore, in what has become the national anthem of that country, "My

Beautiful Bengali Homeland." But the term eludes all precision: this book and all the books any of us could write about home would not exhaust the meaning of *desh*. The most widely read literary magazine in Calcutta is called *Desh*. It refers to Bengali language and culture, its promotion and its exclusiveness. Bangladesh fought its war of independence for the sake of its language and protection of *desh*. Like Hungary and Finland and the newly-reborn Baltic countries, Bangladesh is a land that poetry created. Poetry in its broadest sense—culture borne on language—is an atlas all its own. It has redrawn more maps than warfare.

My wife's family moved to Calcutta when her father was just a child and she has never seen Faridpur. Yet when Bengalis ask her *desh,* the same way I ask new acquaintances where they come from, she says Faridpur. The form of the language she speaks is unmistakably *bangal,* the soccer team her family roots for—and many Calcutta boys die for—is called East Bengal. It is the home of character and attitude; it presumes to stand for traits, for skin tone and intelligence, for sensitivity. My *desh* is a village of poets, yours is a village of *goondahs*. Yours is a nest of avaricious women, of drunken men. All our women are beautiful.

WHEN WE WERE MARRIED, my wife could have wired her father: *his* desh *is Québec*. Take away our genetic brilliance, our ancient culture, our natural grace, beauty, and aristocratic bearing, the intellectual leadership bred in our bones, and Quebeckers are quite a bit like Bengalis. They survive, precariously, on the easternmost rim of the subcontinent called Canada; they are hated, they are nationalistic, they have a language no one else can speak.

QUÉBEC IS *DESH* to five million French-speakers in the province, another million in Canada outside its borders, and another five million in New England who now speak English but still know the name of their grandparents' village.

Lac Mégantic is fed from the south by the Arnold River, named for that ambitious border-hopper, Benedict Arnold. In his early guise as an American patriot in the summer and fall of 1775, Arnold tramped from Maine up the Kennebec to the unnamed river and the unnamed lake, then *down* the Chaudière River in a costly, but strategically brilliant, backdoor assault on the British garrison at Quebec City. Two hundred years later, old-time *canadiens* in New England still say they're going "down to Québec," meaning downstream, because the major rivers into Canada flow northward and empty into the St. Lawrence. The *coureur des bois* tradition dies hard.

Arnold lost nearly all his troops through disease and drowning. His siege of Québec failed despite significant fifth-column activity from inside the fort. (Canadian history in an historical image: resisting the Yanks while actively trading with them the whole time.) Arnold was thus obliged to capture the lesser fort of Montréal on his way back to New York. He was brave and audacious but he didn't get promoted, so he sold out to the British and lived there in retirement, apparently in obloquy the rest of his life. But his expedition linked New England and Frontenac with Quebec City in ways that only a few Indians and missionaries had tried before. In my father's name I claim Benedict Arnold as a geographical ancestor in all his moral ambiguity.

Geography defines my father's life. He was a pure product of old Québec, of a decadent and ferocious Catholicism, of a hard and resistant frontier, of death and cruelty as facts of life, and of the lure of America, the promise of riches just over a mountain ridge. A Benedict Arnold, an opportunist, a self-deceiver, and a con-man. All his life he feared poverty and dying in some private hell of a debtor's prison or a Catholic home. His last years were hell, in Manchester. He feared the death he eventually received, he foretold that death, he begged a judge to release him from it, but he couldn't avert it.

When he died, had I not provided the money, there would not have been a funeral. Had a second cousin of mine, a grandniece, not intervened and found him a church plot and membership in the Society of Precious Blood, his death would have been as unremarked as any infant brother or sister in his family. In the end, the church got him.

MY FATHER USED TO CALL dollar bills *p'yastr'*, in other words, *piastres,* the paper money of New France. There were bars he'd take me to when I was still a child, in Pittsburgh and Kentucky and Florida, where bartenders spoke French and prices were rung up in *p'yastr'*. He was not a man of this century, despite appearances. In those bars I'd meet men whose hands I couldn't surround in a simple handshake, and I knew them to be old boxers, their hands mashed flat as anvils. A striking-surface. Their necks, flaring out from their earlobes. You don't want your head to snap back, son, that's how you lose consciousness. We'd go to those bars to listen to fights, and later, when we still didn't have television, to watch them. Piastres changing hands.

My mother would not permit boxing in the house. Nor could she tolerate, with her love of horses, any kind of western. She could cry at the sight of a man or beast being pounded. She was a brave and tender woman. In Florida she would bake cakes and gingerbread and walk them to what she called "the coloured section." On the streets, she'd ask any "coloured man" if he wanted her to go inside a store—since they were not permitted—and buy something for him. And just like my father, she would find women like her, artistic, college-trained, ironical, progressive, even in the midst of our isolation and desperate poverty. She took me one day to DeLand to meet the only writer in central Florida, Marjorie Kinnan Rawlings, author of *The Yearling,* a book that had broken my heart. My mother was bold and fearless; she found these people.

The conflicts between my parents, and consequently inside me, are not easily dismissed. I cannot say my father was the best of his type, but my mother probably was the best of hers. But under the changed name and American manner, he was as pure an embodiment of a 19th-century French-Canadian who ever lived.

A LITTLE MORE than a hundred years after Arnold's strategic exploitation of lac Mégantic, the Chaudière, where it rises from a rocky cleft on the banks of the lake became the site of Stearns Lumber as well as other pulp, furniture, and paperworks. Mégantic, though remote and far inland, is just another fall-line city with cheap water power like all the other mill towns in New England. Trees were like the buffalo to plains Indians; lumber in its various allotropes, pulp and planks, provided everything for *habitants* like my grandfather.

Apart from my father whose purity is a complication I'm still trying to process, I am the product of tangled loyalties and continual uprooting. I'm a native of nowhere. I do not know where I come from because I have come from just about everywhere. Until the eighth grade I had never gone to less than three schools a year. In the fifth grade I won the spelling bee in Jacksonville, lost it in Winnipeg, and won it again in Springfield, Missouri. The next year I started the fifth grade in Springfield and ended up six months later in the eighth grade in Pittsburgh. Another year, I was Catholic, Protestant, and Jewish. In Springfield, a psychiatrist at Southwest Missouri State tested me and wanted to put me in college in order to save my sanity. But we didn't stay in Springfield, the happiest six months of my childhood, the prettiest town I'd ever lived in, the town where I learned to swim and ride my bike in traffic. My father got a job at Solway's in Cincinnati.

A few weeks later, the only other white student in my shop class attacked me with a steel-backed metal brush. I put my arm up in time to get it shattered—and to save my skull. A white teacher beat me for sneezing in music class—corporal punishment with a thick paddle was the only well-attended activity in Samuel Ach Junior High

School—in order, she said, to show the black kids she wasn't favoring me. "You'll thank me," she said. I was ten years old, in the seventh grade; I'd been advanced two grades in the past six weeks, on the basis of my brief Winnipeg schooling a year before. I knew about formulas, I could write essays with a pen.

In a lifetime of amazing visions in Florida, being sent to the supply room, being bent over a chair, already crying—I had never been struck, no fists, no slaps, no spanking was the implicit bargain in our family, given my father's history—being read the charges, and then being lifted off my feet by a bitter woman's expert paddling, was the least probable, most shocking, and scarring event of my childhood. This was the violation of everything I had lived with, everything I believed, everything I trusted. Adults, especially teachers, with whom I had been on such friendly terms in Florida (they used to visit my mother just to talk, the only college graduates in the town) did not attack boys like me. Injustice I could live with. In-dignity, never.

(There's a whole new literary tradition to invoke here: the books that signal the outbreak of revolution, that trig-ger murder and assassination, not from oppression, but from a moment's inattention, the victim's casual assump-tion of the killer's lesser humanity. In books, people don't kill to avenge brutality; they avenge indignities. We can tolerate just about anything if we know in the final analysis we count for something, however slight. The proof that we don't count at all is intolerable. In *Absalom, Absalom!,* in *All the King's Men,* in *The Great Gatsby,* the motive for murder is not a criminal act, it's a small moral oversight.

In Gordimer's *Burger's Daughter,* the precipitating event in the heroine's decision to leave South Africa and to suspend her struggle against apartheid is not injustice or police brutality; it is the sight of a black man beating his donkey on the road.)

TWO YEARS AGO, I drove back through the Avondale ghetto in Cincinnati and found my old apartment building. I wanted to show my wife everything; I wanted to test my memory, and I wanted a witness to the chaos of my upbringing. If my universe is curving backwards on itself, at least let there be a witness to it. My life is often incomprehensible to me and Cincinnati lies close to the center of its absurdity. Avondale is no longer a ghetto, which at least implies coherence within injustice; now it's a free-fire zone in the terminal phase of failed renewal. Forty years ago the storefronts along Reading Road were crammed with goods and services, a full working community. My classmates studied after school in their parents' shops, they wrapped and weighed the butchered chicken parts, cut the cloth, fetched the dry cleaning, translated for their parents and grandparents. If my heart aches from the transformation of central Florida into geriatric reservations and theme-park infantilization, it bleeds from the sight of boarded-up storefronts, open, weedy lots on Reading Road, and the barren slab of shops anchored by a dingy foodstore and a few darkened offices in what passes as a shopping center.

Samuel Ach Junior High School has been torn down, leaving only a plaque at the edge of a scruffy lot. The statue of Abraham Lincoln that used to mark the corner of the playground now stares over the shopping center where the metal grates are kept down, even by day.

I know my childhood was one-of-a-kind, not at all for its fecklessness—on this restless, errant continent I set no records—but for its lack of coherence. I was a rat in the maze, getting shocked, getting sweets, dark/light, cold/hot, prodded/cuddled, making my way to some eventual light, but no one was taking notes. The researcher had fallen asleep. My life has been pointless, one long search for meaning, which in a life means identity. Sometimes I feel the technicians had forgotten to exterminate me when the experiment was over; I was released back to the general rat population and allowed to contaminate as many people as I could. Whatever lesson my life might impart to others, unless I write about it and can do justice to it, has been lost. Whatever I might have learned is still locked away. I haven't strayed from the shape and contents of my life because I'm still trying to discover what I left behind.

ALL OF MY LIFE I believed that my father was the victim of his passions and his temper, that he lost jobs or resigned from them or was offered something marginally better and he took it instinctively because he was a first-generation American. He couldn't afford to turn down a raise or the promise of a raise. He couldn't resist a deal no matter how transparently shabby. (What other people have is better than mine. There is better than here.) And he heard about these new jobs in bars, he got these tips from other traveling salesmen, the most gullible men in America. He might have been poorly paid, been given bad routes, and been representing bad companies, but he could always improve, he could catch up. Like Willie Loman and Mamet's Shelly "The Machine" Levine, he could always get a new territory, a new listing, and be back on the boards.

He'd sometimes quit a job, blowing up at the boss in the process (part of the ritual: "I gave him hell. You should have seen his face. He begged me to stay and I told him to go fry his ear"), only to show up the next day in a new town at the apppointed address and find there'd never been a job, or never a job for him. We wouldn't hear from him for weeks, but we began the desultory packing, the process of saying good-bye.

"Where should we send Clark's transcript?" the principals would ask. "I'd better write you," my mother replied. I hoped for snow or for mountains, but it usually turned out to be Georgia, Alabama, or another part of Florida. And I would go through the new schools, the new get-acquainted fights. He never consulted my mother, he never had a plan. We seemed like opportunistic scavengers, always retreating back to Canada at the first sign of serious trouble.

Then I look at my own moves which appear to be accelerating. In twenty-nine years of marriage, I never had a plan either, apart from going to Canada. We married on a lunch break—no small thing for a Bengali Brahmin woman in 1963—and our life has been an improvisation ever since. (I'm more stable than my father. In twenty-nine years we've moved only twenty-six times.) Resentment and better pay played no role. Curiosity has always been the motive. Geography in its widest sense; that I would be a different person in a different place. A new place meant the hole in my character, the incompleteness, could be filled up, muddied over. The fear that I'm missing something, that a chance to transform myself might not come again. The promise that each transformation would disclose a hidden identity.

That, at least, is how I always viewed it. At fifty I began to accept that I may have been wrong about my father. What if he wasn't an opportunist? What if he was an innocent, a believer? Like all good salesmen, anyone could sell him a bill of goods; he was self-deceiving as well as a liar. His lies were whoppers—that he was a Paris aristocrat—his truths were elusive. Like most people, he lied for advantage and to avoid accountability. But he also fabricated a life, a fragile bubble of sophistication that worked only because of the gullible and insular company he kept. I think he learned very early that people would use his truths against him. Or that his truths frightened people.

Because my father never shared Mégantic with me, because *he* seemed to have come from nowhere, I fabricated a hundred identities, memorized maps and geographies from the age of five, and made myself at home, on native terms, with every place we ever settled. I've been loyal to a dozen baseball teams, memorized bus and trolley routes in every city we ever lived, studied the street maps and learned the names of every suburb. In my childhood I memorized the radio dial, writing down each call letter, reciting them and memorizing them in the morning, thrilling to the radio-reach of each new city, each new neighborhood. My friends were always the same kind; we grilled each other on call letters every morning. I spent an adolescence listening to Pirate games on car radios that carried us away from clear reception into that ether where crowd noise blends with static. I could tweezer cheers from static and extract a game narrative from the shards of Bob Prince's voice. I could pluck a phoneme from the air and extrapolate the count, runners, and score. In the early years of television I'd carry the rabbit ears to the apartment roof or suspend them out the living room windows, conjuring call letters and test patterns from the snow. To sell me on a move, all my father had to say was "it's got good reception," or "it's up on a hill," and I'd be packing.

I was a good, loyal pooch.

I didn't get it—that each of our moves was temporary for him, but a potential hometown for me. From each six-month segment wherever I was dropped I tried to generate a full life, starting with local sports teams, moving on to the local landmarks and the names and patterns of streets. I saw each new town as the definition of the rest of my life, each new school a chance to shine. But my father had gone to a cheap father-school; he wasn't trained to head a family. He went through marriages like a diplomat changing posts, each marriage a fully absorbing experience with languages, scenes, friends, and stepchildren, followed by a reposting. I had expensive son-training. My duty, I knew from an early age, was to redeem my mother's mistake.

If there is a genetic base to character, and science tells us increasingly it's all genes, then the relationship between a placid, flaccid, contemplative, uncompetitive, nonaggressive son and a father who was mindlessly hyper in all those categories must be subtle indeed. What are the curious inversions wrought by nurture over nature, by a mother's reasonableness over those rogue paternal chromosomes? If I am my father's son, then his qualities should be as manifest in me as mine are (so obviously) in my two sons. But where?

Sometimes the most upsetting judgment about my father that I can reach is simply this: what if he was just like me, curious, driven to put something behind him, optimistic about something, some glow, just ahead? What if he loved us, in his way? What if this legacy of chaos was really his offering, as though to say: *I have given you a taste of everything that was denied to me. I did it all for you, son. I went straight for almost twenty years with your mother so that I could see you grow up; I never understood you or even respected what you did until it was too late. You were not the son I would have chosen, but you were the only son I got.* And what if the corollary is also true: what if I am just like him?

I HAVE MADE MYSELF a native of twenty different towns and spent a life in reconstructive, autobiographic surgery. I'm Canadian—French and Anglo, Montrealer, Torontonian, and Winnipegger; I'm American—southern and northern, midwestern, North Dakotan, Cincinnatian, Pittsburgher, Floridian, Georgian, Missourian, New Yorker, and Iowan. I'm mainstream and ethnic. In the past ten years I've laid out my five-mile running loops from British Columbia to Florida and Argentina, Québec to California and New Zealand, I've registered my cars in five states and two provinces. I'm American-born, an

American resident, and an American citizen, but my books are filed under Canadian Literature. Until the category "North American" is accepted, that's where I belong.

You've got to come from somewhere—everybody does. But I don't come from Fargo, North Dakota, where I was born, or Florida where I spent my childhood, or Pittsburgh, or Iowa, or Montréal. Iowa has been a sheltering presence in my life for thirty years, it is the place more than any other that gave me a life, but it doesn't feel like my home. And so I look for something to cling to: a homeland, a fatherland.

Sometimes I look in the mirror and panic. Who are you? I ask. What are you? This is the longer answer to the question, where do you come from?

The mysterious hold of my father over me is that he is the only purity in my life. He is the essence of a time and place, typical even in his deviations from type. Through him I understand the appeal of racial and national politics, of collective thought, of belonging, of treachery. He is my link to a tribe.

IT MAY SEEM a small distinction, perhaps, entering the money-economy without a safety net, going from share-cropping to log-walking, abandoning the land in favor of a factory, looking for better jobs and higher wages instead of praying for rain, but it's not insignificant for the children who can't turn back.

My grandparents were part of the two great historic migrations of French-Canadians: south and east from the Beauce and the Eastern Townships into the formerly Scottish and British loyalist regions of Québec, and south again, twenty years later after all their children were born and most had died, into the mill towns of New England. In Frontenac in the 1870s and 1880s, before the arrival of the French, Gaelic (*Gaelic!*) was the dominant language of the older farmers, English of the younger. *Le Travailleur,* published a Gaelic page as late as the 1920s. Truly, Frontenac was a land that time forgot.

And my father, whom I fought as a bully, as a coarse materialist, as a man who loved only money and thought only in terms of money and valued only money, was actually something much larger.

He simply collapsed two or three generations of economic evolution into a single lifetime, pushing himself into middle class life without ever touching middle class values. His origins were as modest as Andrew Carnegie's in Scotland or any *shtetl*-born immigrant's son pushing a cart on the Lower East Side and dreaming of uptown emporia. His achievements were, of course, far smaller, minuscule, but no different in kind. He was driven. He was hollow. His single-mindedness, his blindness, his spontaneous misrepresentations, his terror of failure and of dying poor and being buried in some generic Potter's Field were as real as any drummer's, or any plutocrat's in Dreiser or Norris.

In the summer of my freshman year at college, when I told him I'd have nothing to do with his plans for me—running furniture stores—that I'd never pay protection to the neon-sign Mafia or to the Teamsters Mafia, I'd never lie to customers, never cringe before bankers, grovel at Rotarians, and gouge friends, I might have been standing up for values I believed in but I was also attacking him in his only area of confidence, his only unequivocal success. He'd built two furniture stores from scratch. Then he tore down everything he'd ever built.

Reverse-capitalism is a terrible thing to watch, the equivalent of assault and battery on property, the deliberate gutting of an enterprise from sheer hate. If he couldn't pass it on, then no one would have it. The stores had been his family; he'd gotten from them the things a family might be expected to give a man—status, praise, pleasure, a respected place in the community. And when they proved barren, he turned on them.

I remember a vivid image: my father standing at the front door of his store apparently fishing in his pockets for the ring of keys. But he couldn't find them, and he stood there with both hands in his front pockets, and from the street he looked like a well-dressed man pissing on his door.

I didn't understand it back in my sophomore year of college when I came home for the summer to stores that didn't open till past noon, to my mother sitting alone and crying in one store while the other one was locked and dark. I sat in the second store for a few weeks with the lights on and the doors opened out of loyalty, but terrified that customers might actually enter.

And that was the story of my father's great success. My father married the lady he'd been seeing, and denied seeing, a couple of weeks after the divorce—denying till the very end that adultery had occurred—and went to Mexico with at least a hundred thousand dollars. It was an ancient dream of his—Mexico, San Miguel in particular—all from an article he'd read years before in the *AAA*

Traveler magazine. Servants, haciendas, steak, and margaritas in a perfect climate, all on a hundred dollars a month. The marriage and the money lasted less than six months.

I got a picture a few months later, taken by my father in a bus station in Mexico, his head bandaged, face cut up. By then I was married; this was the first picture of my father that my wife had ever seen.

He said his new wife's boyfriend, a Mexican beach-boy, had roughed him up. At the time I didn't believe him, but now I tend to believe the bad things, the few bad things in his life that he couldn't forget or misrepresent. He said his new wife had brained him with an alarm clock and taken off for Texas. He went to Florida and introduced himself to a nephew, my Aunt Bella Lessard's son, Harvey, a tailor in Hollywood. Harvey took my father to a New Hampshire party.

Two weeks later, he was married again.

IT IS A CHILLY, cloudy, windy day in August 1989. The Québec autumn has just descended. The lake is flecked in whitecaps. The Dairy Queen sign flaps smartly in the wind. I have come to Lac-Mégantic to trace my family, to hold those ledger books and read the handwriting of Fathers Cousineau, Choquette, and Beaudry.

There's a small restaurant in Lac-Mégantic, built on a wharf out into the lake. Fishing nets are nailed to the walls, along with lobster traps and sea shells and photocopies of the old Lake Megantic ferry. One might think it a fish or seafood restaurant. On this night, at least, all it serves are Virginia ham and spaghetti with meatballs. The mustard and ketchup and grated cheese arrive in their yellow, red, and green commercial packaging. The question might be, of course, but what did I expect?

I remember the cold, bright summers in Gaspé and the Laurentians, where skinny children sold cans of blueberries picked that morning. I remember the seasonal *casses-croûtes,* camper-trailers with drop-away counters wheeled to the side of a mountain road, and families working the grill and the deep-fry baskets (*patates* from rancid grease, a delight), and I remember the prefranchise, Gaspé version of frozen custard, with a *bombe* of hard ice cream wrapped in paper like a stick of frozen butter dropped down the tube of an ancient machine to be whumped, and belched out the bottom in a giant soft rosette into a waiting cone. *Voilà, m'sieur, une molle à la Québec.*

STANDING THERE in the parking lot of the Hôtel de ville of Lac-Mégantic, I remember how my father ate his ice cream, how he would bite the scoop from the top, even of a Dairy Queen, and never lick it, how he chewed it, never let it melt. My tongue-patterns wrapped around the side; his chisel-marks, down the middle.

I TOOK MY FAMILY—wife and two-year-old son, Bart—fresh from Iowa to Montréal in 1966, an act of longing to find my *desh*. It was an imperialist act, maritally and politically; my wife had no desire, as an Indian, to once again become a British subject. She wept when we crossed the border at Windsor. After her divorce, my mother had gone back to her family and schoolteaching in Winnipeg. My father was, so far as I knew, in Mexico with his third wife. I'd had no contact with him and desired none. All my mother's-side cousins—my post-modern siblings—were in Canada. My aunts and uncles were my surrogate parents. I was the only American in my family.

I was twenty-six in 1966 and dreamed, with my new Iowa degree, of solving all my ancient dilemmas in one brilliant stroke, finding myself and my writing voice in Canada. (At least there'd never been a moment's doubt about which Canada: Toronto and Vancouver were never considered.) The southern stories I'd published to that time were exotic even to me, accidental outcroppings of an unhoused childhood. They excited certain resources of language that came naturally enough, but weren't really my own—they were Faulknerian, incantatory, as though I were speaking an ancestral language I'd learned from a grandparent and had never been forced to study.

In my last year in Iowa, I'd studied with the Chilean master, José Donoso, the first (and probably still, the only) non-native English-speaking author the Writers' Workshop has ever employed. He was also the first foreign writer I'd ever met. Latin American literature had not yet exploded on our shores (except for the nonpareil, Borges); he represented a new empire of expression for the few of us who chose Donoso instead of the other two visitors that year, Vonnegut and Algren. With Donoso, I wanted to bend my world to include something of his, and so I'd begun widening the circle of my writing world, touching on French-Canadians, but placing them in Florida. This was the world I carried into Montréal in 1966, a fragile, damaged eggshell with a sterile chick inside, though I didn't know it at the time.

Despite being insufficiently French, psychologically Anglo, and too much American, I had the arrogance to believe that my life allegorized Canada's national identity crisis. I was a personification of that old British garrison at Quebec City, fighting off Benedict Arnold while trading with him out the backdoor. Knowing nothing of the city, nor of its writing community, I nevertheless dreamed of bringing an Iowa-style writing program to Montréal. (All Iowa grads are proselytizers.) My real dream, I realize now, had been to transform myself into a Canadian, preferably

French, to link up with Montréal as the true son of my parents.

In other words, I wanted to reintroduce my parents to each other, watch myself being born, and write about it. I wanted to bring them back together in Montréal, and be the child I could have been, had they never left.

In those fifteen Canadian years, more of the dream came true than I might have dared to wish. I was a young writer present at the birth of contemporary Canadian writing. (It was like a coffeehouse experience in Paris; everyone together in a single time and place, an agenda to discuss, anthologies to collect, publishing houses to launch, the young getting started, the literary midwives returning from Europe, the friendly journalists crouching at the edges.) In Toronto, at the planning session for the Writers' Union of Canada, we shook each other's hands with the exaggerated respect of self-conscious, self-important young people launching a movement. *Some day,* we must have been thinking, *someone will write of this moment.* (It being Canada, many people have.) We were a literary generation and even though I was still an American citizen, I was one of the designated links between Montréal and Toronto.

(It also contained the seeds of failure. No French writers involved. My wife, a Canadian citizen, was not invited. It was a mainstream, white, Ontario-generated, intensely nationalistic affair with little time for issues other than the American domination of Canadian institutions.)

My wife was hired by McGill the moment she finished her Iowa Ph.D. orals. I was not and spent a year teaching English as a Second Language in McGill Extension. The next year I was hired as a temporary replacement in the English Department to teach modern British and American and creative writing, at Sir George Williams University (now Concordia), the other downtown English-language institution. So was a young poet named Margaret Atwood, who'd won the previous year's Governor-General's Award, while still a graduate student at Harvard.

Bart, at three, used to run down the hall of the English Department at Sir George Williams University to Peggy's office, where she kept cookies for him in her drawer. Our second son, Bernard, was born that year and slept in her dresser-drawer when we went to her place for dinner. Over lunch one day she admitted that she'd also committed some fiction and asked if I would read the manuscript of a novel called *The Edible Woman*. She thought it might even get published if she could line up British and American publishers to go with the Canadian.

Now, when Ph.D. students working on the Margaret Atwood papers come across that early manuscript in the McMaster University Library, they have to ask me for permission to quote from lunch-hour doodles, unkind queries, useless advice, question marks and exclamation points on the margins. It's another form of autobiography, the unballing of paperwads. Nothing in the universe is ever lost.

I stalked the streets of Outremont and NDG checking out the landmarks in Hugh MacLennan's and Mordecai Richler's novels and in the marvelous documentary stories of Hugh Hood. Our kids lined up at the grill for Alice Munro's hamburgers, and we went to the ballet in Paris with Mavis Gallant. Mordecai Richler came back from

England and settled nearby. Margaret Laurence was back from England. George Bowering was a softball buddy. Michael Ondaatje and I bounced around the country, co-winners of a national prize, giving readings to snow-trapped librarians on blizzard nights. It was possible to know everybody.

For a few years I was able to read every new book of stories, every novel, every issue of every literary magazine that was published in Canada—it wasn't that hard—and with four of my friends, John Metcalf, Ray Smith, Ray Fraser, and Hugh Hood, I gave readings in every Montreal English-Catholic high school. We tailored our stories to a high school audience, making them local and fresh, a challenge to the Chesterton and Belloc, Garner and Callaghan in their anthologies. And finally I convinced a skeptical chairman and a dean ("you propose turning out writers like Ford motorcars?") to let me start a graduate writing program.

MONTRÉAL WAS RAPIDLY TRANSFORMING itself in preparation for Expo, and then its wake, but the old city that had defined my parents' world was still in place: my mother's old socialist friends from the 1930s, the first generation of McGill women professors, still taught. The founding fathers of Anglo-Québec writing and law—Hugh Mac-Lennan (his *Two Solitudes* is one of those novels whose title shorthands a time and place or perhaps an entire society, like *Gulag* or *The Grapes of Wrath*), and Frank Scott, who could be thought of as the Thomas Jefferson of Canada—still hung out in their florid-faced corner of the

McGill Faculty Club. Women professors still had to enter by the rear—lest they overhear ungentlemanly language—until the new generation of American-trained academic women, Myrna Gopnik and Bharati Mukherjee, and others, demanded an end to it.

What I'm suggesting is that Montréal, even in the late '60s, still spoke as my personal intellectual and literary center of the universe. These were the names I'd heard of at home, the authors I'd sought out in libraries and read with a kind of proprietorial interest that exceeded their literary merit. MacLennan's *The Watch that Ends the Night* evoked a Montréal that my mother knew, the communist idealism of a Norman Bethune, the McGill doctor who marched with Mao. Her old friends on the faculty knew MacLennan quite well and offered to arrange a meeting between us; I was shy, but agreed. He totally rejected the whole idea. Canada was still an authoritarian society in many ways. My ideas of literary friendship were American in general, Iowan in particular. Communitarian, accessible. Whatever their democratic convictions, the old guard were social crustaceans ingesting Scotch directly through their carapaces.

Before she'd found work at Eaton's in the mid-'30s, just after returning from Prague, my mother had baby-sat for Frank Scott. The little boy she put to bed is now a major poet and senior colleague of my wife's at Berkeley. Over at Concordia, my chairman was Neil Compton, *Commentary*'s television critic. His apparent full-time engagement with pop culture suggested a life of robust enthusiasm and cool detachment. No one outside Montréal knew he was chairbound by polio or that his writing issued from a pen-cartridge attached to the second joint of his right index finger, the only muscle in his body that he fully controlled. His successor, Sidney Lamb, was the CBC's jazz critic, and an old friend of Johnny Gallant, a jazz pianist at a local hotel-bar, and first husband of Canada's greatest writer and permanent Paris exile, Mavis Gallant.

Canada had its achievers. Northrop Frye, Marshall McLuhan, Glenn Gould, and Zubin Mehta, demonstrated Canada's *panache* in the worlds I valued. Leonard Cohen, Neil Young, Joni Mitchell—white soul, for a while, was a Canadian specialty.

Pierre Trudeau, the intellectual heir to Frank Scott's legal reforms, was the Prime Minister of Canada. For a few years we were living under a philosopher-king. Uniquely in democratic history, the most intelligent, most qualified person in a country had also risen to lead it. For a few years, I felt myself in cosmic alignment: my past and present had come together, my fictional world lay just outside my door, my professional life was devoted to the thing I most wanted to do: discover talent and help to train it. I remember those fifteen years now as an effortless time and a kind of grace period.

The Canadian world that I'd chosen to make my own was sufficiently new, and difficult, to keep me reading and learning. But sometime in the first six or seven years, my French stalled out, it reached a level of proficiency but not of fluency, so that I could not improve upon it without surrendering totally to an east-end life in a French university. We spent our summers in India and Europe. We rose through the academic ranks, our books appeared. For the last times in our life, we were both tenured full professors in the same city.

Perhaps it's inevitable, given the morganatic relationship I've established with two dozen possible hometowns, that the only home I feel comfortable claiming is the only one I can never possess, whose language I'll never speak perfectly, and whose citizenship I had to work for, and then give up. My home town is just about the only city east of the Mississippi where I never went to school and never spent a day with my parents.

In the late '70s, after years of budget-starvation at Concordia, I accepted a similar position at York University in Toronto. It should have been culmination; instead we were done in by the racism. In 1980, at forty, we left for the United States.

WHEN MY FATHER was forty, in 1945, he gave up the only security he'd ever known, the low pay of furniture-buying for Sears in Pittsburgh, for the South. First Atlanta, where he started a showroom, and then central Florida, where he started a furniture factory of his own. Ambition and warmth, history and geography, must have driven him: he knew wood and carpentry. The South made sense, he knew the country was tired of war and ration cards. My mother designed the furniture; he sold it. Lee's of Leesburg. The factory was taken away because it was successful; the bank exercised a buyout clause. He went back on the road selling, then had the devastating accident. After his recovery, he moved us around the South at six-month intervals.

Our arrival in north-central Florida, not the Gold Coast, was a miscalculation, like a stage-struck midwesterner heading to Broadway and stopping in Trenton. Or the Hollywood-bound landing in Barstow.

So many things I remember. His only vulnerability, the way his joints would swell minutes after turning a screw or assembling some furniture; how proud I felt, handing him his carpenter's tools and knowing their names, soaping the screws, how I'd whack at the nail with a hammer, bending it, how all his nails went in with one blow and a second tap. How his cheeks would billow with effort, the puff of breath, the tobacco smell of his sweat! Like a modern ball-player, all he needed was a draining of his wrists and knees after every strain. He never exercised, never worked out, and he was a much older father than any other I knew, but he was the fittest, the most athletic. A bullneck, barrel chest, biceps like grapefruits, veins like blue baling wire, an upper body that belonged on a six-footer, all squashed down on a five-six frame.

Watching him as I did, inspecting him for clues of my own insufficiency, it seemed to me our bodies were enacting some comic inversion of inheritance, some ultimate joke on the gene pool. Both my parents were splendid specimens, they deserved something better.

I grew up with allergies and flat feet and daily headaches. I was paunchy and waddling, but turkey-necked, hollow-chested, pigeon-toed, and spindly-armed. Any unaccustomed walking during the day sent me into fits of nighttime agony, and the need for metal arch-supports to be tied tightly around my feet. I drew pictures with my feet and picked up marbles for exercise. I wore high-laced leather shoes in a rural southern culture of bare feet, endured the inevitable fights, and—because of allergies—slept with a wet cheesecloth over my nose to breathe through. Still I dreamed of success in baseball and football, listened to all the games, memorized the names and statistics, dressed in a flannel baseball suit my mother bought me and red satin numbers she sewed on the back.

"You can be number 11," she said. "It's easier for me to sew."

I'll know I've gotten old when—in the emptiness of my house or office—in front of a mirror I no longer wind up and fling a curve ball to myself.

A baseball memory: my father taking me to my first game, in Venetian Gardens, Leesburg. Class D, Florida State League. Teaching me the scoreboard and the stats, and buying a little book of Florida State League records. Being left-handed, I looked up left-handed records. Most wins by a left-handed pitcher: 24. "Remember that name," my father said, "he's famous." It was Stan Musial. It's remained my favorite bit of baseball trivia.

Of all the places I've ever lived or visited, I could return most willingly to Leesburg. If the organism is destined to die in the place of its birth, as my parents nearly did—Winnipeg to my mother's Wawanesa, Manchester to my father's Lac-Mégantic, I'd choose Leesburg. Or maybe one of those cinderblock, lakefront cottages between Leesburg and Tavares, living on fish and book-reviewing.

"ELLE A SURVÉCU!" I say to Madame Beaudoin, the town clerk of Lac-Mégantic, who patiently photocopies each ledger page for me and has been growing depressed over so much death. She survived! After two days of photo-copying family births and deaths, I've finally found the birth record of an aunt, Bella, who lived beyond her childhood.

She became Bella Lessard, and I remembered her from a visit to Manchester when I was fourteen and it had looked, temporarily, as though we would go back to Montréal from Pittsburgh to settle. Bella was a widow, the smart and gracious one in my father's family who wrote us on holidays, the only member of the family with whom my mother corresponded. The other survivor in Manchester, my Aunt Lena, sent us envelope-cards for mission support in India and China which my mother tore up.

My father's latest blowup had gotten him fired from his buyer's job at a failing downtown Pittsburgh department store. (Rosenbaum's; it's now a parking garage.) The week that I slept on her sofa under the crucifixes on every wall and plastic bleeding heart as a nightlight, was one of the lowest weeks of my parents' married life. My father feared an assault charge. He was waiting for a phone call from his trusted young secretary: if the police were called in, we would flee to Montréal. And that would have been my new life. I chose, a dozen years later, to make it my life. And I've written about it incessantly. My father had done it once before, in 1935, fleeing a wife and an assault charge in Manchester for Montréal, and there he'd met my mother.

Apparently he'd walked into his cubicle-office in Rosenbaum's and found a stranger sitting at his desk. "Clear out your desk, you son of a bitch," the new buyer commanded. Rosenbaum's had just been sold to a national chain, the new buyer came from the New York office with orders to liquidate the stock, pronto. My father did not a have a golden parachute. He knocked the man through the cubicle wall. That week we spent in Manchester and I met my aunt for the only time in my life, I didn't know that we were fleeing the law, fleeing Pittsburgh—and maybe the United States—and that we had absolutely nothing. We had fled the apartment and our furniture.

In an earlier book, *Resident Alien* (1986), I imagined a life that went north into Montréal, based on such a premise. A totally English-speaking boy from Pittsburgh with the name of Porter is launched on his northward course—*le chemin de son père*—by his father's violence. His father suddenly starts speaking French. One day he's a Pittsburgh teenager, the next day he's literally sleeping on an uncle's floor in Montréal—a city and an uncle and a language he'd known nothing about—and starting his life over, as a Carrier, in a French school. He becomes a total border-crosser, a murky undefined consciousness. But that was autobiographical fiction. In reality, we only visited Montréal for a week and my father showed me Le Chez Son Père where he'd been a singing waiter. We drove the wrong way into a one-way street, and he joked with a cop, *"mon erreur,"* and I was amazed that he actually spoke the language, that he could unravel the mysteries, that he belonged. All of it has stuck. He poked around a few furniture stores and told us things in Canada were hopeless. We were going back to Pittsburgh. He was fifty, and within a few months he'd signed a lease on the old Scandinavian restaurant, which we restored, and Blaise Wayside Furniture was born.

I'M THIRTEEN YEARS OLD, in our first year in Pittsburgh. Down on Liberty Avenue, in a coffeehouse, I sit with a young, very nervous Italian girl, my father's secretary at Rosenbaum's. She has lustrous olive skin and a full bosom, a blouse with frills down the front that accentuates it. Her bright lipstick and bright earrings make her pretty in a villagy sort of way. It's like a date, I think, though I'm still four years from my first date, which will be in college. She is on a date.

She's smoking; that's very sexy. Fine hairs on her upper lip, heavier hair, like an outline, running up her arms. Unbearably sexy. We're touching here on powerful themes.

"Lee said you collect stamps," she says, and I'm about to answer, "British American only—" in my stupid, too helpful way, when she pushes a mounted Vatican panel of—what else?—famous pope stamps. Ornate, a little tedious.

"I thought, since you're Catholic too . . . ," she stubs out the cigarette. I don't deny it. "The Holy Father gave us an audience, you know. I mean, a bunch of us from St. Joe's. He saw all of us." She looks at her watch. "I don't know. He said he'd meet me here."

FOR TWO DAYS in the back room of the City Hall of Lac-Mégantic, I track down the family, copying each birth and death, learning the family names of all the collateral relatives, the *parrains* and *marraines*—godfathers and godmothers—and their relation to the family, noting the names of the various witnesses to deaths and births, identified in the records as cousins and uncles. By marriage I am related to all the Lamontagnes, Chouinards, Roys, Paquettes, Richards, and Nadeaus in Lac-Mégantic. It gives me, at fifty, a sense of rebirth into a new family, as though I have been adopted by a tribe.

And of course, I have. The *québécois* are a tribe, identifiable by the French they speak, old and proud, polluted and corrupted, and by their sheer tenacity. The price they'd paid for their survival. Recognizable by their intensely French *métier*-names, nearly untouched by immigration, suggesting their pre-Revolutionary origins as porters (Carrier), millers (Meunier), furriers (Pelletier), bakers (Painchaud), and butchers (Boucher). In France during the Revolution, peasants discarded those hated caste names and adopted less constricting identities. But the Revolution in France never touched New France, which was a British colony after 1763.

A garrison society, then, not a colony, holding the fort against erosion, seeing all temptation to assimilation, to worldliness, to business, or any welcoming of unions and large-scale immigration as a threat to the collective family. The real oppression—shame for betraying the race, for deserting the language and the religion—came from within, not from the Americans or the English-Canadians.

Sitting in a back room of the City Hall of Lac-Mégantic that August, looking back a hundred years, I felt like a Faulkner brooding over his Yoknapatawpha. The sudden arrival of new families marrying into mine, new witnesses to births of doomed babies, the first relatives able to scrawl their names as witnesses. I imagined the ever-pregnant, ever-grieving women, the stoical men, the professional mourners and witnesses. The rituals seem Asian, or *shtetl,* comic and exuberant in the midst of so much grieving.

The family names spread, all French, as Lac-Mégantic slowly replicates the directory of names from the limited repertoire of founding families, until one day in the 1890s when a word appears that practically pops off the page: *Frydmyn.* A marriage. Eliezer Frydmyn, son of Sophie Grynzpyn. But the poor priest, trying to spell out that vowel-less tangle of Polishized French, goes through five lines of crossings-out. Never has he encountered such a name, such a country—Pologne—and the girl he's marrying is a *fille mineure* (a minor) accompanied by her father and several brothers, all of whom can sign their names. One can imagine the hunting rifle resting on papa's lap.

So Eli Friedman, itinerant from Montréal or down from Québec, perhaps a purveyor of dry goods for the farm girls of Frontenac, or perhaps fresh off the boat and boat-train and mistaking Mégantic for Montréal, takes a fancy to a 15-year-old, knocks her up, or perhaps gets too friendly in other ways, or perhaps is smitten. Whatever the case, it's a happy resolution, a Catholic marriage with fathers and brothers very present. The imagined movie-director becomes Woody Allen. When the gypsies arrived in *One Hundred Years of Solitude,* for better and worse, the isolation of Macondo was broken, the vision of the world was set clearly before them and then there was ice, and the banana groves, and death, war, starvation.

In just twenty years, a generation, Mégantic grew up. In my father's first eight years, the population doubled from 1,173 to 2,259. When baby Rolland, the eighteenth and final child, died in 1909, my father—a boy singularly at odds with piety, devotion, or obedience—became the *donné,* the designated priest. The only education he ever received was at the hands—often literally—of the Sacré Cœur fathers until he walked out at the age of eight when the family left for Manchester, never to study again.

He never reconciled himself to the church. "I'd sooner kill the sons of bitches," he told me once when (in ignorance) I'd suggested he see a priest. I wasn't thinking of religion. I was thinking of having someone for him to talk to. This was in Pittsburgh when he was waiting for my mother to come back to him after she'd left him permanently for Canada.

I began to infer brashness, timidity, intelligence, from the sudden appearance of signatures. Overnight, it seemed, the town turned literate. There are no photos, but I could almost see them: moustached, unsmiling, small, hard men. The signatures suggested the faces behind them, and the photos from Gold Rush camps, Civil War battles, artists' ateliers. Amidst the groups of anonymous young men in droopy moustaches, young women in bustles, so much a part of their time, suddenly erupts a modern face: a time-traveller, our contemporary with knowing eyes, our hair, our smile, our clothes and posture. You want to address that picture (or in my case, the signature): *you! How did you get back there?* That person can't be dead! Those dynastic faces, transcendent of their time and place, letting us know: *we had our good times, too. You're not so special. We passed on our genes.*

The names blended, illiterate "X's" and the same professional mourners like Joe Laroche who never missed a funeral, until, in 1897, a new uncle arrived on the scene, François Chouinard, who signed as the witness to the death of his infant daughter, Blanche. He is married to Rose Délima, Achille's sister—my great-aunt—and his signature that sad day is properly frail and autodidactic, an old man's sprawl except that he must be young.

THE ONE TIME I asked my father the names of his childhood friends and of his—my—relatives, he mentioned only two. A Charlie Gagnon in Manchester and Frank Chouinard in Canada.

A YEAR LATER, signing the ledger as a witness at the birth of my own aunt, Blanche (who died herself before the year was out), he took up a full line with a sweeping signature, bold as the priest's himself: *Frank Chouinard.* Frank! He'd changed his personality. Baby Blanche is buried four times that year and born five times to other aunts and sisters. *My Aunt Blanche Chouinard died four times the year of her five births.* That's how Márquez does it, he simply reads the papers, and suddenly German girls die of gunfire on the fourth of July and babies are born five times.

It was a decade of massive self-transformation after all, the first years of the CPR, the first decade of Mégantic's existence. Did François ride the rails and go to the States and become "Frank"? (I can hear those American workers. "Hey, you, Frenchie. Fran-swah." That's a potent Frank-maker.) Did he come back to Canada and spread the gospel of American riches to the family? I wonder if I am looking at the signature of the man who changed my father's life. I see Frank as the first shape-changer, the first charmer, the first role model in the family.

The difference between birth and death is a priest's say-so, his record keeping. Birth and death are literary events. Resurrection is merely a revision away. Burying and christening a dozen children on a cold winter day, or in the septic summer months, Father Beaudry returns by candlelight to enter the records, beginning each entry with the family name, and then the date, and takes four or five identical lines before inserting the happy word *baptisé* or the pathetic *inhumé* into the unvarying formula. By then, the priest is nodding in fatigue. Joe Laroche and the happy or hapless father are shifting in their seats. The wind is howling or the mosquitoes are biting, the horses are restless. Rushed, the priest momentarily forgets, and crosses out a birth with a death, hoping the father can't read or doesn't notice.

I MAKE A COPY of every birth, every death. Finally, it is 1905, time for my father. Here, in the elegant handwriting of Father Beaudry, my father is born (in my translation):

> The twelfth of February, 1905, we, parish priest undersigned, have baptized Joseph Léo Pierre Roméo, born the previous night, son of the legitimate marriage of Achille Blais, day-laborer, and of Orienne Boucher, of this parish. The godfather was Pierre Richard and the godmother Césarie Blais, cousins of the infant, who, except for the father, have signed with us.

and compare:

> The sixth of December, 1892, we, the undersigned priest have buried in the church cemetery the body of Joseph François Homère, who died two days ago at the age of eighteen months, legitimate son of Achille Blais and of Orianne [*sic*] Boucher of this parish. Present were Joseph Laroche and Achille Blais who have not signed.

In one terrible summer week in 1898, the deaths of baby Achille, three years and ten months, and five days later Orianne Blais, three years and a half... twins, it would seem, unless the priest forgot their names and confused them with their parents'. Who would know, or care? My baby aunts and uncles, all mowed down before my father's birth.

In the August week of 1888, with the Megantic Outlaw on the loose, my family buried 4-month-old Marie-Alice Blais, a niece from Longue Lac, Maine, then on August 24, Joseph-Alcide, eight months old, and before the week was out, three more. Five children, all under the age of five. (Two-thirds of Benedict Arnold's troops had also perished of the swamp-borne fevers of the region.) I had heard of this calamity from my mother as a kind of distant but unthinkable tragedy—like a Bangladesh cyclone in its implacable bleakness—but because the story had come originally from my father, I'd also discounted it.

Québec Catholicism tends to canonize the children who die: I think of Marie-Claire Blais's *A Season in the Life of Emmanuel* and of Jack Kerouac's *Visions of Gerard,* two books steeped in the popular Catholicism of Québec. My cousin Grace of Bensonhurst, whom I met too late when she was already dying of cancer, mentioned going up to Mégantic only once, to put flowers on the grave of the saintly baby Rolland. She never forgot that when she looked for the graves of her aunts and uncles, all the babies who'd died, she found nothing. To her, the bones were probably heaped in a pile in an unmarked grave.

CHAPTER THIRTEEN

THE LEDGER BOOKS suggest a principle for dealing with my father: he was a naïve liar, not a fictionizer. In later years I'd even doubted the eighteen children—but he's right. And the deaths, he's right again. He fabricated only flattering things, absurd overreachings about wealth and education that in retrospect are almost endearing. If the story made him look good, it was probably a lie. If it was intolerably sad, it might be true.

No other family makes the same number of appearances in the parish ledgers. Even in those toxic and backward times, we have manured the cemetery with fallen children, as Faulkner might have said. Were these sickly children doomed by the same mysterious condition that even followed me and my aborted siblings, or were they all as strong as my father, potential boxers and hockey players, doomed by the medieval sanitary conditions, or accidents, or violence?

This is God as child abuser.

Is my family especially cursed, or was it a special sense of frailty that propelled the two surviving sons, Oliva to France and Léo to the farthest recesses of America outside the pull of that fatal gravity? What sense of grace, or guilt, or destiny devolves upon male survivors when they beat such odds? Yet Mémère, who died just before I was born, and the two surviving daughters, my aunts Bella and Lena, all went to Mass every day. The daughters married and never left the same block in Manchester where they spent their next sixty years.

Perhaps the question is best put positively, Darwin-like: not what disease killed fourteen, but what qualities saved four.

In certain cultures—Brazilian Indian, for example—where infant mortality is even higher than in old Québec, the mothers apparently refuse to bond with their infants for the first year. The infants are neglected by our standards, but it is a form of psychological self-protection. Perhaps my father was a survivor because he didn't need love. Perhaps he became a self-contained monster of rage, turning to endless numbers of women to replace the mother who wasn't there, an intelligent child who never received and never returned love as we understand it.

Going through the Lac-Mégantic ledger books, I had a sudden sympathy for the grown-up adopted children one reads about these days or sees so frequently on television—thirty- and forty-year-olds seeking genetic consolation by finding their natural parents. They say they're worried about inherited diseases, thus trivializing an honorable curiosity. Every poor *québécois* of my generation whose relatives were born or died at home, unattended, is adopted in that special quasi-medical way. I know nothing of my father's relatives, not even why they died. We have the names and parishes of our ancestors but no history. No autopsies, no comforting descriptions of their talents, their personalities, their appearance. Where no reason is given, fate is the answer.

When the state takes over, we begin to get answers. My father's first wife divorced him in New Hampshire over "fear of mortal injury." He died, they say, of an embolism brought on by hardening of the arteries.

AND SO I CLOSE the ledgers, say good-bye to Madame Beaudoin, and walk in the cold breeze along the lake. Out there eighty years ago, my grandfather walked on logs with the cant hook, and in the winter he skated out of sight, arms extended under the buffalo robe. More memories from my father, the only time I asked him about his father. He also said he was very tall, which again I took as exaggeration, since his sisters and one brother were less than five feet tall.

The parish priest, Father Sirois, offers to introduce me to Mr. Stearns, manager of the condo development that has replaced his family's lumber mill, but I forgo the pleasure of balancing the ancient social *décalage* between our grandfathers. He takes me instead to visit the other Blais family in Lac-Mégantic, Jean-Marie, the retired hardware-store owner. ("They're very Catholic," the priest confides. "I'll introduce you and sneak out early.") Primed with all the family names, I quickly establish my bona fides.

Jean-Marie is the grandson of Louis Blais, Achille's brother. We are second cousins. His bearded young son, a pharmacist and true *québécois,* third cousin to my sons, has brought his family out for a visit from Montréal. This son—not Jean-Marie who is tall and red-headed—looks very much as I had imagined my character in *Resident Alien,* a true son of Québec with all the proper political attitudes.

I am their cousin, name spelled wrong and French a little faulty, but forgiven. The proliferation of names, of children, of wives, the stiffness introduced by the unannounced appearance of a priest, all distract me from my real intention.

Tell me, I want to say to Jean-Marie. *You're sixty, I'm fifty, we're men of the world, and this is your scene. You're as close to the source as I can get. I can't talk to my father, and my cousin Grace is dying, and Lena is senile. You're the only one left. My Mégantic griot, my Chicken George and Kinte. . .*

But he's serving tea, playing with his grandchildren, and this is not the time to ask about the baker's dozen of dead babies and what he knows of my father. He's heard stories about the wanderings of my grandfather, his Uncle Achille, who left first for Maine to find work ("Bates Shoe, in Lewiston," he says), then to the inevitable Amoskeag Mill in Manchester. He knows that my father went to Florida and had a son but he'd heard the boy had died, and after Florida the story is lost. I've just resurrected myself, for which he is glad.

THE ONLY SURVIVOR of my father's generation is my Aunt Lena, now 92, widowed and childless, whom I visit in her nursing facility on my way back to New York. I've never met her, but the moment a nurse introduces me, she clings to my arm, running her fingers across my face. "Yes, yes," she says, "it's Leo."

Stephen King meets Thomas Mann in those cold wooden barracks with crucifixes on every wall, an ex-tuberculosis sanitarium on a fog-shrouded mountaintop in central New Hampshire. Her life has been shrunk to the contents of a single room, one dresser with standing photos of her long-dead husband, who was Irish. None, unfortunately, of my grandparents, whom I've never seen. Deaf and too vain for a hearing aid, she begs me to take her away. "They torture me," she cries. "They starve and beat me." I remember the mission envelopes she'd sent us, the pictures of churches in India with big crosses over the doors and priests with their hands on little boys' shoulders. A good thing my wife had never seen them. My aunt looks healthy, if unattended, twenty years younger than her age.

She calls me Lee. I've become my father, at last.

It's the same old Catholic medievalism, I comfort myself. They can't be beating and starving and torturing her. But it's an interpretation to comfort myself, not my aunt, an excuse for me to pull away. Those words, *torture, starvation, beatings,* they're an equivalent to something beyond language, I think. They have to be or else I'm like my father, an unfeeling monster. But what if it is all true? What if I am hearing the voice of a time-traveler, and age has merely loosened her from her fears and pieties? Freud refused to credit his patients' reports of child-abuse and incest, blaming the victim instead. Maybe I'm sparing myself the pain and refusing to listen to her.

In her world, senile and deaf and Catholic, I can't separate metaphor from reality. I remember the "blessed" children of Trinidad, where blessing comes from *blessé* meaning wounded, and to beat means to bless. I remember the beatings administered by Greek parents to their children on the streets of our old Montréal neighborhood. There, too, I resisted breaking them up. (Immigrant parents love their children, I kept thinking. This is a ritualized form of love. It has to be.) I remember having to shield a little girl in our apartment building, Anastasia, who liked to burn our letters through the mailbox grille, and my fear for her life if I ever mentioned it to her father.

My father, too, when he spoke of his childhood mentioned only the beatings from his father and the priests, and he became a boxer in self-defense. With him beatings were a slight injustice—he accepted the beatings as proper to his sins and a properly painful price for the luxury of walking out of the church, guiltlessly. Beatings create the sins to justify them. In later years, he was grateful for the beatings. In polite company, meaning in front of me or my mother at the store, that's what he'd talk about with his Irish and Italian friends: whose nuns and priests were tougher, meaner, crueler.

Is my aunt telling me now the literal truth—was she born to a world of beatings, married to beatings, and now suffering from attendants' beatings even into her old age? I have no one to ask and no way of learning. I waited too long to contact my aunt and my cousins. I'm dealing with smoke and a suggestive word or two.

Mémère, my father's mother, lived one summer in Montréal with my parents soon after their marriage. She thought my mother, a foot taller than she at five-feet-eight, a giant. My mother remembered her mother-in-law fondly as witty and good-humored—everything my father wasn't—despite having lost fourteen children. *Catholics don't value life the way we do,* my mother reasoned. Mémère had lived in New Hampshire for twenty-five years and spoke good English. She'd gone to Catholic schools in

Sherbrooke and learned to read—a marriageable skill. (Boys were too busy with important work to learn such things: pépère was illiterate.) She would arrange candles in a semicircle on the floor around herself during thunderstorms. She went to Mass every day. One day she asked my mother a question that stuck with her all her life and would take on resonance in the years to come: "Why did a good woman like you marry a boy like my son?"

ON THAT SAME TRIP down from Mégantic, after seeing my aunt in New Hampshire, I stopped in Wethersfield, Connecticut. It's now just a southern suburb of Hartford, first turn off the interstate. The address on the 1925 marriage license between Leo Blaise (he'd added the "e" by then, curiously, but kept the first name) and Delia Chartrand is Walcott Hill Road. I'd imagined Walcott Hill as an old-time, self-contained ethnic neighborhood. Sixty-five years later, I surmised, it must be plowed over, or "redeveloped" like the other ghettos we've lived in.

But Walcott Hill Road is Wetherfield's main street, the first road parallel to the interstate. Walcott Hill Road: my father lived here—or at least came here and didn't return to Manchester—between 1926 and 1932. He walked this street a married man, a young French cock in a cloth cap and attitude, when he was younger than my sons. No address was given, so I drive its length, pausing for ice cream. The area has been leveled in that antiseptic, resentful way of grant-generated renewal. One might think a malevolent occupying force decreed this destruction, the way Communist authorities defaced their own cities in the name of anti-bourgeois purification. But this is my personal history they've destroyed, a chance to touch something he'd touched, or even to see something he'd seen.

Standing by the car, eating, I see a tawny apartment-block across the street, the only remnant of the old, mill-town Wethersfield where the immigrants, French-Canadian in those years, must have clustered. I can imagine the clotheslines, the powerpoles, the sidewalks alive with children, the streetcars linking Hartford and New Haven, Boston and New York. *Ragtime,* of course. And I see I have been chewing the ice cream, my teeth marks make twin ruts and with a narrow median strip between them.

COUSIN GRACE, who was twelve at the time, remembered being told by her mother, my Aunt Corinne, "don't ever go over to Uncle Leo's alone." When I ask why sixty years later, she says only, "A boy shouldn't be told bad things about his father." "But I'm fifty and you're seventy-five," I say, "it's okay, you can tell me." But it's not okay. Even though we're sitting in her Bensonhurst house and she's been married fifty-five years to an Italian immigrant and she's now dying of cancer, we're still in her parish and parish politics rule.

"He was supposed to go crazy around women," she finally says. "Then there was their baby boy—"

"My brother," I interrupt, wonderstruck. I'd heard they'd had a stillborn son, but that rumor, too, had come from my mother on the night she'd told me of his first marriage. According to my father, the baby boy had died in birth, crushed by his mother's abdominal muscles, be-

cause she'd been an Olympic swimmer. The blame, therefore, the denial of a proper young bundle of physical
attributes, fell on her. The wonder is not that the baby
momentarily existed, but that another of my father's claims
is actually confirmed.

"No," my cousin corrects. "He was your father's
boy." A Catholic distinction, Old World. Only children
of your mother are true brothers or sisters. What's a father?
"He was born dead."

My mother, lost in her last ten years of an Alzheimer's
fog in a Winnipeg nursing home, retained only her English
manners, the nurses said. (It would have been nice if she'd
also retained her diamond ring.) She responded to their
feeding her and cleaning up after her with tact and a helpless
gentility. From her salad of Alzheimer words they could
always extract, "I'm sorry" and "this is terrible, daddy,
simply terrible."

Transformed utterly, she was still herself: considerate
and ashamed. Others on her floor retained the core of their
personalities—the randy old men pinching the nurses and
exposing themselves, the censorious old schoolmarms
clustered at the elevators in their wheelchairs to be the first
to attack a visitor for not taking off his boots. A core of
truth must remain, I tell myself now. My mother's breed-
ing and good manners. My aunt's beatings and starvation.

I think of my mother, now five years dead but nearly
twenty years beyond recognizing me, thinking of me as

her father, then not registering me at all, and I remember our Florida years, how she'd walk up to black women or men, or even children on the streets of Leesburg asking them if there was anything they wanted her to buy for them. She would take down the names of truckers, of waitresses, bus drivers—anyone of exceptional kindness or efficiency—and offer to write letters to their bosses for commendation. In the towns of central Florida, she was a foreign freak—a college graduate, a foreigner who'd traveled to Europe and spoke languages. She gave interviews in Florida weeklies attacking segregation as an offense to decency.

The pain those moments caused me, the literal pain of being attacked as her son in the schoolyard, the humiliation as she talked on the street with black ladies, or made me walk with her through "Niggertown" carrying gingerbread cookies. She could ruin a movie for me by whispering the rumor that an actor or actress was Republican. Their credibility immediately crumbled. I became her life, the sole justification for the mess she'd made of things, what she'd thrown away. I was the prize she struggled over, my soul, my talents, my loyalties and decencies. She won.

That such fineness should be lost, it appalls me. Every death means the world must be reinvented.

I THINK OUR PAST never dies, and our future is forever claiming its place. I believe memory is but a form of futurity. My memories are pushing me forward.

We are born whole, we fragment, but we try to recompose. Our younger son was only three years old when he started drawing the usual child-house-tree stick figures, but with a slight addition. Under the house and the child were squiggly lines. "Worm roads," he called them, and it was the pattern of unseen roads, not the usual tree branches or curling smoke or airplanes that occupied his full attention. He grew up to be an archaeology student.

WHEN MY WIFE and I lived for a year in her joint-family in Calcutta, relatives used to seek me out for special attention. "See that woman?" they'd ask, pointing to a plain, pleasant, and outwardly virtuous relative, "she had an affair with the doctor." Of another: "She is sleeping with the landlord's son." Of another: "He got the job through blackmail. He discovered the boss is taking bribes, and threatened to expose him. . . . " On and on it went, a year of the most outrageous and embroidered rumors, or stories, or truths, that left me suspicious of every new family member, every well-known businessman or politician I met. I felt I'd entered an older worldview, pre-electronic and pre-journalistic, even pre-psychological, in which the bottled up disapproval, or jealousy, or disillusion, or envy, that eats away at families imprisoned by poverty in the socially mandated confines of the joint-family, could only be projected through gossip.

MY FATHER REMEMBERED *pépère* without affection as a log-walker, the fearless man with the long "kendog" (cant hook or Peavy) for spiking the logs and turning them over, who walked hundreds of yards out into the lake unjamming logs with his kendog as they drifted to the mill. (An old Québec joke: if a man is going to drown, shout out, "Save the kendog!") To me, Achille Blais, the walker on water, the skimmer of ice under a buffalo robe is a legend: father of eighteen, founder of a line, frontiersman, smasher of 300 years of primogeniture and rural passivity. Perhaps a wife- and child-beater. He, and not my father, is Pedro Páramo. A stubborn, brute life-force.

Which means my father's life was a reaction to his father, to his seen and unseen influences, to the dead siblings who must have exercised a terrible presence-as-absence—a ring of little Plutos, perturbing the gravity in his family. A childhood among the ghosts—what can it be like?

III

IN

MY

FATHER'S

HOUSE

THERE IS SOMETHING DARK about my father, a shadow on his character. This is the disfigurement that I defined myself against growing up, one of the few certainties in my life: *I'm not like him.* My mother, who never stopped loving him and fearing him, even after a cruel, deceitful divorce and his two subsequent disastrous marriages, nevertheless called him a sociopath. She'd read his character in a *Readers' Digest* article, "Are You Married to a Sociopath?" As in all things psycho-poppish, the answer was clearly, "yes, you are."

Of course these were the innocent late-'50s, years before Ted Bundy gave a bad name to sociopaths, and this was the *Readers' Digest,* our bathroom reading during my growing-up; they didn't want to frighten their readers. Sociopaths in the '50s weren't serial killers. They were just moody and unresponsive, and they could be helped.

She brought me that issue, with her underlining: *Yes!* and *Lee, to a Tee!*

She was right, it could have been a portrait of my father. Is he charming to strangers? Does he easily gain their confidence? Good God, *Digest,* what do you think a salesman is? Have you caught him in fabrications? She'd never detected him in an unguarded truth. She was forever learning from customers and friends of his French birth, his heroic, highly secret service in the French Underground, his medical training at Harvard. Ah, the crash of '29, how he'd been forced from medical school to look after his family. His eyes would mist. A burden to shoulder—he came from such a large and talented family, you understand, and despite the aristocratic background, the ancestral lands weren't as productive as they had been . . . So he'd abandoned his dream of medicine and law and saw his brothers and sisters through music schools. He'd been forced to take over the management of a chain of furniture stores—Canada and Mexico as well as the East Coast. He'd sing for them, "La Vie en Rose" or "Around the World," and after my parents separated, he would find my mother's phone number and sing into the receiver "Are You Lonesome Tonight?"

Does he have a temper?

A violent temper?

Is he subject to moods, to violent shifts of mood for inexplicable reasons?

Does he retain friendships? Does he have a sense of loyalty? Does he have any friends he can count on?

My father had cronies, no friends. Even his cronies would come to my mother and say, "Lee's very lucky he has you. He'd be a bum without you." Once our store was started, he asked me to spread the word among my high school friends to have their parents come to us for any furniture. The parents responded and my father immediately jumped the prices. Once *borax*, always *borax*. Our banker told my mother even before their divorce, "Without you he'd never have gotten the loan. Your husband frightens me." Our doctor said, "I treat him for arthritis, but that's not his problem. For that he needs a different kind of doctor, understand?"

For the twenty-odd years of her marriage, she lived with thirty moves, insecurity, lies, rude, surly, and unfaithful behavior. The quiet companionship of marriage—shared interests, conversation, confidences, understanding—these things were outside his competence. He worked obsessively hard; he paid bills, he fantasized enormous private dreams of wealth. He died a week after talking to me of again starting a little store, something he could handle without having to walk.

And what have I learned about my father in those thirty years? I have learned that categories, even categories of pathology and psychological labels are discreet: yes, he answers to the description of a sociopath. And also of a mutation, a broadjumper through time and space. His lies are my fictions; his silence is my verbiage, his tribal markings are my longings for a homeland. He had no friends, he was destructive, violent, cruel, incapable of loyalty or sympathy with other people, incapable of love but endlessly demanding. I look back on it now and think—given all he went through, the currency of denial that purchased his survival—that "sociopath" is too harsh a term. He'd lifted himself into the middle class by marrying a woman he couldn't talk to and having a son who embarrassed him. He was not a serial murderer; he was Jay Gatsby.

I wonder now, giving him credit, if his outrageous claims of aristocratic birth were not his defense against my mother and her background, her education and European travels, the taste and style and eye she brought to fashion, to friends, and to furniture. Left to his instincts, my father was pure *borax:* pink and black sofas with silver threads.

The cronies with whom he drank after closing and "fished" for long weekends were other Catholic "boys," Irish and Italian, which really meant no Jews or WASPs with whom he felt uncomfortable. No one ever visited us. In the twenty years of our life together, we never entertained at home, we never cooked or served for other people. The patio was never used, the dining table never set. The den and wet-bar, the downstairs bedroom and bathroom were decorated for parties that were never thrown. The framed plaques and pictures, those outrageously happy faces of my father and his friends taken at furniture conventions, with many women in low-cut dresses, bore nothing of our life, nothing of the man I knew.

We had one extraordinary souvenir, worth by now untold thousands of dollars. It rattled around our drawers through many moves, I held it, even debated playing with it. Then it disappeared in one of the divorces. In 1952 or so, during the summer Furniture Convention in Chicago, my father had won the All-Star pool. The prize was a baseball sent down to the dugout and signed by all the old-timers. It was a baseball, surely the only one in existence, with Musial and Schoendienst, but also Cy Young, Pie Traynor, Connie Mack, and Honus Wagner. When I want to torture myself, I think of that all-time all-star baseball in someone else's possession or perhaps merely lost. I think also: this is the mark of the life we led and the family I come from; we touched immortality once, and we didn't recognize it and never really valued it. Anything fine that ever comes to me, I will lose by fire, theft, or accident.

My father had no intimacy, no conversational gifts. He was a showman-*manqué,* a performer who faced the world of strangers with something approaching a script and a terror approaching stage fright. Each encounter demanded a fresh cigarette; he could not leave the house or greet a customer without lighting up.

When I think of the innocent pleasures I take in hours of conversation every day, the ease of teaching, the collegiality, the repartee, the married banter, and the faith I've placed in language, the sheer ability to alter reality by describing it or lampooning it, I begin to realize something of my father's life-sentence. Each time he talked, it was an assault, a small-time breakout. A man like my father—distrustful, abused, uneducated—must learn to talk. Language is a female medium, a churchly function. The "silent type," that American stereotype of masculinity, must oftentimes mask its opposite: violent insecurity. In my growing-up, my father could maintain a silence through a weekend, sleeping in nearly till suppertime every Sunday.

My only strength is the ability through language to re-invent the world at will. My father cried when I read him portions of my book describing parts of his body he'd never noticed. He looked down on his chest, touched the little nodules on his nipples, the scab near his navel. Without that ability, the world must be a terrifying place.

His culture placed no value on education, only on obedience. He drove Montréal whiskey trucks into the States during Prohibition, dropping off the cargo in Troy.

A French-speaking boy with few scruples and fast hands had a role to play on those dark mountain roads in Vermont and the Adirondacks—lonely, unlit roads blocked by fallen timber, hijackers and sudden shoot-outs. In my father's life is written the ethnic subhistory of the great northeast: Jews in Montréal brewing the liquor, French-Canadians driving it in, bribing the sheriffs and handling the hijackers, turning it over to the Irish middlemen in Troy and Albany who took it to the Italians of New York.

The sons of all those liquor-handlers now write and film their fathers' stories. William Kennedy, the Albany novelist, sat down with me one night and rattled off all the names, French on one end and Italian on the other, with his favorite Albany Irish criminals in the middle. American male culture, a love of sports and a love of crime.

AT THE MANHATTAN JAZZ-PARTY where I met the Tavares woman, I overheard a private investigator with an Italian name, complaining, with proper indignation, about WASP assumptions.

"Everytime the insurance suspects a Mob hit, they give me a call. Jeezus, I tell them, you think I know things the cops don't know? Why's that, huh? Cause I got an extra vowel on the end of my name?"

On my next pass, a few champagnes later, I mentioned I was working with a private detective in New Hampshire trying to secure my father's police records. This time he was more interested. "Yeah?" he asked. We talked of the liquor-running. "You wanta meet an old-time Mafia Don? My uncle, he ran the whole fuckin' liquor business on the

West Side. Hadda lotta business up in Troy. His wife's still alive."

"GYPSIES, TRAMPS AND THIEVES..." sang that Armenian-Cherokee princess, Cher, setting a new standard for California beauty back in the '60s though we didn't recognize it then (my sons, too, are part of an unplaceable, Portugal-to-Punjab American look). And now the echo of her old song comes washing up, "...Kikes, Frogs, Micks and Wops...and every night their men would come around...and lay their money down."

Even in Iowa City, at a dinner party thrown by Chinese doctors, the wife of a Dean tells me a story of growing up in Chicago, in Tony Accardi's neighborhood, a friend of Fat Tony's daughter. Her mother worried about her going to the daughter's birthday party. "It's okay," the little Mafia princess said, "the Chevie's bulletproofed."

WHAT I'M REMEMBERING is simple enough: ethnic lives embrace duality. In Cincinnati when I was eleven, the only other hillbilly in the class—meaning the only other white gentile—tried to kill me. He was a psychopath, and I was weak and unprotected. After that (my left arm was shattered at the elbow), the school said I had two options—leave or integrate.

My father was for discipline, a Catholic school or a military academy. In his world, my bandaged arm was the badge of my incompetence—of course "they'd" try to kill me. I was asking for it. For him, the fact that it was a West

Virginian was irrelevant; I was among enemies at every turn.

The school, and my mother, took a different view. I was slow and fat, white, and smart. That meant, in Avondale in the early '50s, I was a Jew. If I didn't want to transfer to St-Somebody's, or a generic marching school, I had to join a group. And so I was taken to the Temple at the top of my street, introduced to a young rabbi, and enrolled in Temple Youth. Back in the seventh grade, my classmates were a couple of years older, already smoking, already learning their letters for their bar-mitzvahs. They worked in their fathers' or grandfathers' shops after school, and so did I, happily, gratefully. Clark the pantspresser.

I had a community, I listened to the grumbles of my friends, about the rabbi, about community politics (it was the McCarthy period, and the Avondale School Board, which was almost by definition socialist and communist, was one of the first institutions to fall), and I pressed pants. I was sent out by the local Temple to sell Marta Schlamme tickets. The neighborhood, Avondale, was half Jewish, half black, and the lines of habitation were not clearly demarcated. There were even some black Jewish kids in my class. We looked for mezzuzahs on the doorjambs, announced ourselves loudly in Yiddish, but not all Jews hung mezzuzahs, and many blacks, when they moved in, failed to remove them. We had to be clever, sniffing for food odors, listening to music ("Barry Sisters, I hear Barry Sisters!"), knock on doors, and be prepared to run. It was like trick or treat, hide 'n' seek, kick the can, all those expectant, bladder-burning games of childhood in a grown-up world. Some of my classmates had actually been

born in Europe and survived the Holocaust, and they believed to be caught in the wrong place without protection
meant certain death. Calling on my old skills as a deep
South entrepreneur, figurine-seller to Yankee tourists, I
even sold Marta Schlamme tickets to blacks.

My father was working at Solway's Furniture downtown. We were a pair briefly, my father and I, learning
Yiddish curses. But while his experiences always taught
him the permanence of his isolation, the bitterness of the
barriers between him and management, and wiliness and
unaccountability of the *borax* world, mine—just a degree
or two off his compass—taught me who I was and where
I should be.

CHAPTER FIFTEEN

THE HOUSES OF MY CHILDHOOD were always rented. There was a house in Fargo, an apartment in Cincinnati, a house in Pittsburgh, and then, starting in 1946, rooms throughout the South. Some vital function in our life was always shared, kitchen or bath or often both. On South Street in Leesburg we again had a house, in Tavares the cottage, and then more apartments, every year in every town and city until 1957 in Pittsburgh when, at 52, my father finally built a house.

I am typing this sentence on my fifty-second birthday.

A House for Mister Blaise: built on so wild a gully that deer came up to feed in our backyard. We had a patio with a brick barbecue, decks off the master bedroom with a master bath, a gaslight out front, a double garage, a flagstone fireplace that divided the living room and dining room, although no one ever dined there and no family ever lived there. An address, Robinhood Lane, in a development named, of course, Sherwood Forest. We never fired up that barbecue. We never lit our fireplace.

That house was like the old Chrysler Town & Country convertible, a luxury waiting to claim him, to wrap him in the wreckage of vain, ostentatious glory. He was a salesman, and his sense of accomplishment was driven by trophies, by plaques to hang and pictures and a plastic accordion of credit cards and fake badges he could flash. Lodges, clubs, names to call on, cards given out, cheap-looking women he could escort. The waiters who knew him, the reservations he could command, the free tickets that were given, the tab he could run. A house was something different. A house required occupancy, settledness, an end to roaming.

That was the pinnacle from which we immediately began to fall. The house, in the remote south hills of Pittsburgh, became my mother's prison. I remember the winter nights of my freshman-year Christmas vacation, cars spinning up the hills, trumpeting like elephants on the ice.

Where's dad?

FROM 1945 UNTIL 1950, we lived in the South. We left Jacksonville in 1950 (Market Street, back apartment) for Winnipeg. Canada was the curtain that descended between the acts of my parents' lives; 1939 (Montréal–Fargo), 1945 (Pittsburgh–Atlanta), 1950 (Jacksonville–Springfield), 1954 (Pittsburgh–or what?). And in 1966 I launched the Fifth Canadian Act, moving my young family to Montréal and staying in Canada until 1980.

In 1950 we settled in two upstairs bedrooms in my grandfather's house in Winnipeg: 1306 Wolseley Drive, between Stiles and Raglan, on the steep terraced banks of the Assiniboine. I was enrolled in Wolseley School and told, like all Americans, I'd automatically be put back two grades. My relatives were powerful people in Winnipeg and their pride was hurt; a sixth-grade tutor was assigned instead. I'd never held a pen (all our work, even arithmetic, had to be clean-copied in ink, using a standard nib on a standard stem, dipped in the well at the upper right corner of our desk). The Florida schools I'd attended had ranged from the appalling to the dreadful, from one-room shanty-cars for migrant workers to the last white outposts on the edges of segregated outer space.

My grandfather, the old doctor, the Luther Burbank of Western Canada, the crossbreeder of Chinese and Ontario plums and apples, the importer of Clydesdales, and father of the modern Canadian insurance industry, was—unlike my mother in her final years—utterly despotic and utterly demented; he roamed the house tyrannizing my grandmother and my mother, confusing one with the other, therefore threatening me for hugging my mother and especially rearing up before my father like an enraged grizzly whenever he ventured down the stairs.

"You! Out, sir! I said out!!" he'd bellow. Short, dark, smoke-shrouded, oddly dressed, undeferential, my father would stare him down, confident that the rage would pass along with the memory. "Morning, Charlie," he'd say, "good day for a walk, don't you think?" Outside, the Manitoba winds were blowing, hoarfrost tinkled in the incredible cold. Upstairs, my father would sit by the window, smoking by the slit he'd cracked open, eating from a plate of cold cuts my mother or I had smuggled upstairs. When my grandfather would see us with a plate of food, he'd swipe the plate from our hands, complaining of waste, of smugglers.

Ten hours a day my grandfather, the man I'm said to resemble, would sit in the living room with a dull pencil and a stack of newspapers and old magazines, underlining every sentence, his single-mindedness, his mental energy as focused as ever. The guardian of his house, the patriarch, the Protestant God in my mother's firmament.

THE ONLY TIME my father ever visited France was in the summer of 1977. He got his passport from the Canadian Consulate in Boston, despite having spent the better part of sixty years in the United States. We'd been in India for the year—my wife had headed a Canadian cultural institute and I'd written *Lunar Attractions.* He'd had his vascular surgery while we were away. He was seventy-two and utterly helpless, a keen mind and an avid set of eyes. His wife considered the French insistence on using their money a calculated insult to American currency, and so refused to go outside.

He was an old, dying colonial in imperial Paris, a city he knew surprisingly well. He knew the districts of Paris from some mysterious osmosis that had also taught him Charles Trenet and Edith Piaf songs, the "Marseillaise" and the other detritus of empire. He arrived in a wheelchair, ready (if I did the pushing) for weeks of sight-seeing. He had to leave after five days in pain so deep it made him cry, his feet dead and frosty; as cold as his face when I touched it in Manchester a year later. I pushed him around our Paris apartment, then down the Vaugirard, and onto the Metro, up to the top of the Tour-Montparnasse so he could see the Paris he'd talked, and knew, so much about. And that was it, the culmination.

I want to think in his last year that he developed some sort of interest in a larger world, that he actually read a book or two including one of mine, that he gained the beginning of a perspective. He knew he'd been a failure and that he deserved no respect from me, but he also knew I could still give it. He tried to reach out to his grandsons, but the wearying battles with his last wife had left him silent in her company, and nearly anyone else's. He'd lost the power or the will to speech.

I read him passages from *Lunar Attractions,* then still in manuscript. Sick passages in a way, a son's scrutiny of his father's body, a son's fascination with the forbidden knowledge of masculine adulthood, a world he feared he would never reach or understand. The microscopic scrutiny of his legs, his chest hair, the black silk stockings, the garter belt, the Arrow Darts with the collar-bar. During that year in New Delhi as I'd walked across the trashpits and through the neighboring village for my nightly tea, I'd been composing my father through all the avatars of our various houses, squeezing all the love and dread that was in me.

The epigraph to that book was taken from a poem, "The Film Maker to His Father," by an old friend, Frederick Feirstein. The part I'd quoted went:

> . . . No matter what others take
> For intellect, art; I know
> That for each illusion I make
> There is one scenario:
> It's our unresolved debate
> About where love must leave off
> And how much freedom to take:
> That's what my craft contains.

He'd forgotten to bring with him (or deliberately neglected bringing) the names and addresses of his numerous
nieces and nephews—more of my unmet, unknown cousins—his dead brother Oliva's brood of Paris proletarians.
I'd been looking forward to one final family reunion: my
father, the youngest of the family was now the oldest
survivor, the chairbound patriarch. Since my father rarely
forgot anything, I assume now he was too ashamed—of
his condition, his French, or perhaps of me—to put out
the call.

I HAD VISITED Oliva myself, back on my first visit to
Paris in 1962, when he was seventy-two. I was working
in Germany as a volunteer in a daycare center, helping
look after the children of east-zone refugees while their
parents worked. One weekend I took my German Student
Card and hopped a cheap train to Paris, feeling enormously
sophisticated, a kind of proper son to my mother and the
memory of her great Wanderjahre in the '30s.

He was a tiny, rotund man, five-three, with a face so
like my father's that it was disconcerting. He was living
on two pensions in 1962—French and American (he'd been
a Paris fireman and a translator for the American Army in
1917)—and his apartment came free for serving as a watch-
man. The apartment stands out to me as something permanently squalid in the soul of France, something worthy
of Céline at his most splenetic. In a small exclusive glass
tower of architects' offices just off Place Wagram in sight
of the Arc de Triomphe and the beginning of the Champs-
Elysées, behind a stucco wall and heavy metal door open-

ing onto a landscaped brick courtyard full of gleaming Citroëns and Renault 3000s, my uncle and aunt had their basement space. A gas burner, a wooden icebox, and dirt floors, permanently puddled. He could at least stand straight, but I had to stoop. One of his sons, a first cousin, was there, hiding out. All of France was ready to go to war against itself that summer. My cousin, a proud jungle fighter and veteran of Dien Bien Phu, then a colon in Algeria, was hiding out and fearing for his life.

Many years later, that cousin's young son, a teenaged radio repairman, visited us in Montréal with a Vietnamese girlfriend in tow. He'd heard someone in the family had married an "asiatique" and he wanted my father's and my blessing for his intention to do the same. This was the boy I wanted to see again, and the story I wanted to catch up with, but my father pretended not to remember.

I PUSHED MY FATHER back to the plane. I spent my weekends that fall and winter visiting him in Manchester, in the duplex built for him by one of his very competent contractor-stepsons. Better sons than I (one of them on his way to a million dollars); the right ones for him.

And at the beginning of 1979 I visited him that final time in a French funeral home, meeting more of my cousins for the first time, Lessards from all over New Hampshire and Massachusetts. And I touched his transformed face (the ears, it seemed, had stretched out Spock-like, the lips had pulled thinner, and the nose, God, the nose had receded from its full Roman arc, leaving enormous nostrils like disfigurements from whatever angle I viewed them. The holes would all widen, air would claim him). It was a gray, icy day. Firemen were hired by the parish to carry the coffin. A niece had donated something, he'd been admitted to the Society of the Precious Blood and so the church had gotten him as it always does in that *petit coin du Canada*. Afterwards I went out drinking with his wife's sons—my brothers at last—the contractor and the truck driver and the truck driver's wife who'd taken a practical nursing course in order to help him in that final year. I haven't been back.

AND YET, and yet, I want to say, I have cried rarely in these past twenty years, and three of the times have been over my father. Once was on December 30, 1978, in Toronto when I got the news from his wife that he had died. It was a casual call: "Oh, you're there, I didn't have your number. Your dad died a couple of days ago. You better get here, we're burying him tomorrow."

Another time was a night several years earlier, in Pittsburgh, when he'd begged me to bring my mother back to him. She was working downtown and living in a dingy bed-sitter in Castle Shannon with widowed, divorced, and various kept women waiting for their lovers' calls. I was just out of Denison, back from my German job, and waiting to enter Iowa. One of the younger, underutilized women in the house offered to demonstrate a Saran Wrap and rubberband condom she was sure would work. It was a time of moral shambles.

He'd taken a room in a Pittsburgh boardinghouse, a kind of halfway house for old alcoholics and derelicts, the hall of coughs, with liquor bottles on the windowsills. They called him Frenchie. He wanted to make a good impression on my mother, but he also wanted her pity.

The other men sat half-dressed in front of television sets, their lives and bodies on display, not even glancing up as we passed by. His was the only closed door. I knocked. When he appeared, fresh cigarette lit, silk dressing gown pleated over his pajamas, he took in the vision of my mother and collapsed on her coat, clawing the Persian lamb, body arched with sobbing. "I'm so lost, Anne, it's awful!" and for the first and maybe only time, I believed him.

In those few weeks when he tried to clean himself up, sitting in the downstairs parlor of my mother's boarding-house ("That's your old man, Annie? Really? He's not so bad. I'd grab him myself, y'know?"), I saw the face of a sociopath, or at least the face of my father that the banker and doctor knew and feared. He'd fallen off the high-wire, and there was nothing to sustain him. The monsters he'd always feared—poverty, Potter's Field, the poorhouse, cops, jail—they were all around him. Disease, addiction, begging: the only thing that stopped him was his vanity. The black silk socks and the garter belt, the trimmed moustache, and the fresh cigarette to meet the challenge.

BETWEEN THE TIME that my father left his third wife, somewhere in Mexico, and married his fourth, somewhere in Florida, he got back with my mother. It was 1963. I had just married; what a confusion it must have been for a well-raised Brahmin from upper-class Calcutta. At least she could telegraph her father: *I have met his parents. They're together.* This month.

His plan this time was a new store, out in California. Lee's Interiors, something small and high-class. He'd cured himself of *borax* and fast women. Something in Marin, an idea that might have come from some other article, like the *AAA Traveler* that got him into his Mexican trouble. And so they drove out to California to scout property. My wild, unmarried, Bohemian parents. And when they were out there, something happened. Some straw that broke her tolerance.

If the experience of my fifty years now means anything, I guess it was this: an indignity. She'd spent her life believing that she counted in his life even if he betrayed her at every turn, and now she had the proof that he had not changed, he would use her and discount her importance. He had not changed, he could not change. He didn't love anyone. The next thing I knew, my mother was in Winnipeg, the car was in Chicago, and my father was in Pittsburgh. And I was in Iowa City, with a wife and a baby.

They had gotten back to Pittsburgh, and she'd given my father the slip, driven to Chicago, left the car at O'Hare, and flown to Winnipeg. My father was still expecting her. He didn't know. She asked me to go to O'Hare, pick up the car, and drive to Pittsburgh, to the boardinghouse where she'd left her belongings. Pack the car. She'd come to Chicago to pick it up.

I would have to tell my father he was on his own—she was not going to be fooled again, and she didn't trust herself around him.

When I got back to Pittsburgh—my last visit to that city until called back for a reading long after the memories had died—it was to that same boardinghouse. But the moment he saw me alone, he knew there'd be no resettlement in Marin, no "Lee's Interiors." His face collapsed, he fell to his knees and grabbed my legs. He wasn't in his bathrobe, just his pajamas. He had not shaved, and he smelled of all his years.

"I'm not a dog, you can't throw me out on the streets. I'm not something you beat and beat..." I was crying with him, toppled next to him on the floor, wanting to be away from all this, to be a man free and out on my own. "She's gone back to Canada," I said, and each word was like a separate stabbing, the way he flinched and shook his head as though to deny it.

CHAPTER SIXTEEN

I REMEMBER the near-panic I felt in those unreal, post-Easter, warm weather buffer weeks of April and May, as my high school summer loomed ahead, and I once again became "the owner's boy" down at the store. Every summer I entered my father's world, and it was brutal. Driver's helper, uncrater, deliverer, occasional salesperson, bank-depositor, general *schlepper*. I'd survived a childhood of schoolyard abuse in the south for being northern and slow and fat, and in Cincinnati for being white, and even in my father's store I was not safe—sooner or later the new driver would discover that insult, drinking, provocation, propositioning the housewives, and finally stealing from them when their backs were turned would not meet with instant sacking or retaliation. They'd push a little further, saying to the housewives we delivered furniture to, "the boss's little boy here says you put out for the drivers. What d'ya say? He'll wait in the truck." To assuage her outrage, he'd dress me down in front of her, "You little liar, you shit, you *told* me...Look, ma'am I'm really sorry about this..."

The supply of the insolent, stupid, lazy, unemployed, or recently paroled in the Pittsburgh labor pool seemed inexhaustible. They were motor pool vets from the Korean War and Teamster dropouts accustomed to dropping furniture or gouging it with their rings, smashing neon signs, intimidating small-business owners into paying a commission for each undamaged delivery. Their strength, anger, and violence matched my father's, but they lacked the wattage of his smile and his salesman's charm. I was caught in the cross fire. My father maintained control over them by being louder and more profane, more prone to convulsive anger and greater unpredictability.

He stood up to the goons. His fears were elsewhere.

HE FEARED HIS FATHER, the man with the spiked kendog and violent temper, who beat him. The Brothers in the monastery beat him. He despised the church, not as a lapsed Catholic, not as a principled opponent, but as a Saracen might, as the Ulster Constabulary might, as an almost mystically pure gutter of the creed might. He stored a lifetime of sins, bit back a ton of confessions. If a revolution ever came, he would be among the priest-killers first.

He feared my mother, but with a fear that forced him to sneak around her.

How like the stereotype of a modern Hispanic my father appears to me now—entering the country fists-first in a low-weight division, coming and going illegally, using his temper, the rage, the charm, the macho, the untrained intelligence. And leaving this country just as suddenly, deserting his wife in the process.

What are the conditions that would lead a man in 1936 to leave a wife and a livelihood in the United States to return to Montréal and the life of a commission salesman?

Rule out nostalgia. Prohibition was over. The only answer that makes sense is that he was fleeing prosecution, perhaps for wife-beating, maybe for something more.

"Arrest a Frog for wife-beating in 1936 in Manchester?" a local policeman snickers. "You kiddin' me or what?" All the New Hampshire police records from those years have been wiped off the books. I'm too late to know.

MY COUSIN GRACE remembered Uncle Léo and Delia in Manchester. She even knew her sister. Delia, according to Grace, was a big, dark woman. The Manchester City Directory of 1925 calls her a shoe-worker, living at home with her father, Henri. My father was living with his parents and listed as a hardware salesman. Why would they go to Connecticut to get married?

In that New World, medieval Catholic currency of Québec and Franco-America every man is presumed to have created a shadow-family. It's part of divorcelessness, of male entitlement and female submissiveness. The gene-tree of any community would tell a different tale from its official registry. There are two sets of accounts known to all, but only the church record survives. In communities where everyone looks basically the same, no one's too tall or too fair, no sudden genetic quirks spoil the cover. No one probes too hard. Relationship runs through the mother's side, inheritance through the father's name.

Which is to say, any sixty-year-old or older in interior New England, short and swarthy, could be my brother or sister. When I'm in Manchester, or in Québec, I see my father everywhere, small dapper men with moustaches.

Which is only to say, I'm barely part of a regional tribe. It's comforting to know there's a place for me and embarrassing to me that I have no claim upon it.

AT THE OPENING of *Pedro Páramo,* the first stranger in Comala turns out to be a brother. "You're looking for your father? He's my father, too." Shared paternity is a truth acknowledged, but does not confer brotherhood.

LOOKING BACK NOW on my adolescence, I can begin naming my father's lovers; they were the women who worked for him, the customers, the bank tellers, the waitresses, the family friends, even the friends of my mother and the mothers of my friends. Many times I would find myself being driven to a suburban house or a downtown apartment and being introduced to a girl or boy roughly my age but of no conceivable sympathy, who would take out a pack of cards or a board-game like Monopoly, while my father and the mother "went shopping." If every stranger is a brother, every woman is a former mistress.

CHAPTER SEVENTEEN

THAT'S WHAT HIS LIFE IS NOW, static on an old car radio, pulling in the ballgame, the songs, Jack Benny, and Walter Winchell, the big-city voices at night as we zipped across the neck of Florida to the ocean. . .

Picture a man, now fifty-two, standing on a beach. As a child in Florida he'd been taken to the beach to clear his nose, to give him a chance to sleep on stuffy nights when his hay fever reacted to subtropical mildew. The warm, moist breeze of a Florida night in the late 1940s remains his favorite time and place, the time of his starting out, the time of being Adam in a world now totally vanished. The world of his imagination that can never age or decay; it is as vivid to him today as it was when he was seven.

He remembers the flash and crash of breakers in the dark, the heavens split apart by the Milky Way. Generations have been born in this country who've never seen the Milky Way, never smelled the ozone of just-liberated oxygen. His special terror, those nights in his mother's arms, propped against a cool sand dune, came from the heavens themselves, the darkness of spreading clouds blocking out the stars and the fear that the Atlantic itself was rising and a tidal wave was roaring in that would lift them and fling them back to Leesburg.

In his memory, the family is still together, the car with the radio shows, his father singing, his mother holding him. How effortlessly he remembers all the lyrics to those songs, because those were the songs his father sang. In the '40s, he was a genius, a gifted child born to ordinary parents. All children, perhaps, are gifted. He thinks about the purity of these memories and realizes that the subject matter of every book, fiction or autobiography, is corruption.

Now, the tide is coming in, carrying everything back to shore. After fifty there are no more coincidences, no more surprises. After fifty everything is probable in a clear, mathematical way. The millions of separate sound-bites, the hands shaken, the hours spent in planes and parties, the books and articles read, the countries visited, the conferences, the dreams and waking fantasies, all the movies, all the television, the radio, the songs, the friends and strangers, the sports and lovers, things written and things heard, the hundreds of spiral notebooks filled with random thoughts, phrases, observations, the business cards and addresses, the arrival of the mailman every day, the pile of letters sent out each day, the phone calls, the fleeting connections made and forgotten—they all mount up and begin to link. That's the meaning of fifty-two years; he has left the world of surprise and wonder and entered the time for answers. He can no longer claim innocence or surprise.

The universe, for him, has ceased its expansion, even when he finds himself, as he often does, at its very edge. Tonight in New Zealand, tomorrow in San Francisco, two days later in Buenos Aires. His travel is a literary dropcloth

over the surface of the earth, a tribute to jet travel and a
corporate card and a mandate to meet all the writers of the
world. A subtle contraction has begun. He's met thousands
and taught hundreds of younger versions of himself still
on their outward voyage, still on their one-way tickets.
He's using up his return.

MANY YEARS AGO, when I was a child and my father
was far younger than I am now, everything seems to have
stuck to me. The memories laid down early are like the
lakes and paths and creeks of the Florida landscape I knew.
Every shovel-strike brought up water. My memories pool
to the outline of their deepest depressions, the smells of a
Florida night, the heat from cracked concrete underfoot,
the fishy smell of large lakes, the sense of promise with
each toss of the baited hook, the sweet hibiscus blooms
black inside with ants and gnats, the sour purple muck too
acid for growing things, and a thousand other sense
impressions that must have bitten and stung me at the time,
to remain so vivid after forty-five years.

My father would drive us, I would sit on his lap in
those straight, barren, Florida roads, and steer. Florida was
empty, more cows than people. It's more than the simple
purity of childhood; it was the vividness of an overloaded
palette spread before me every day. My memories are
happy. No one had died.

THIS IS WHAT I KNOW of autobiography: there comes
a time in everyone's life when accumulated contradictions

take their toll. Chaos mounts: the *out-there*, call it fiction if you're a writer, takes up residence *in-here* and becomes autobiography. Fiction is freedom; a walking away from origins, using what you want and leaving the rest alone. What remains is autobiography, the connections that make your life, but not your characters' lives, meaningful. In autobiography, you grapple to accept the origins and to surmount their limitations, if you can.

I AM MY MOTHER'S SON in strengths and deficiencies. Yet the fascination comes from my father, *le chemin de mon père*. What are the vestigial structures he willed me but were never transmitted? Are they still in me, buried, waiting like diabetes or Alzheimer's to declare themselves?

My mother was never anything but a Canadian, with the proper magazines following us, the *Macleans, Readers' Digest, National Geographic,* and *Time*. She, and not my father, would seem to everyone the foreigner. In Leesburg we lived on South Street, an unfortunate location for a prairie Canadian accent. Before the days of direct dialing, all calls went through the operator. The telephone numbers were 3-digit, plus a color. Three-fourteen Blue. But the operator couldn't understand my mother's Canadian accent. "*Sooth* Street? Where's that at? Don't nobody speak English there?" In our Florida years, she'd turn the telephone over to me.

Just off Route 441 outside of Leesburg, my father leased an abandoned war-time emergency airfield and took the buildings for a furniture factory—Lee's of Leesburg started on a loan, with hangars for storing lumber, the conning tower for an office. I operated the button press. On a private airfield, with runways dying in the woods and gators stretched out in the sun like fallen eucalypti, I learned to ride a bike. I had miles of private roadways, no bullies sticking palm fronds in the spokes. My mother bought the floral material. The woods were blond and silver fox, limed oak.

He lost the factory. He lost the car, the houses, the all-time baseball, the furniture stores, my mother, me.

VERY LATE AT NIGHT my father was at his best. I mean very late—two, three, four in the morning. So was I, when the Deep South streets and town squares were empty and the lights burned coldly through funnels of bugs. These are Florida memories, my earliest, Leesburg, Tavares, up to Gainesville and over to Jacksonville.

Driving cars all night and selling things, usually furniture, by day, that's what my father did. Five days a week he needed no sleep, too busy making good time, six hundred miles a night, shave and a gargle in a gas station, to be parked out front of a steady buyer, top down, at nine in the morning. Those amber balls clipped to the steering wheel, later outlawed, by which salesmen steered one-handed, with the left elbow propped outside, getting burned. Naked women under the amber, you could buy them in any gas station. Naked women everywhere, *hey, kid, take a look:* in rings, in the bottom of coffee cups. Free maps. Spotlights. Dim your lights or get a blast of spot between the eyes. They'll outlaw the spots in a year as well.

He had a way of following the action. We'd stop for gas, sometime after midnight under a Pure Oil or Cities Service sign, and he'd wander off to use the bathroom, he'd say, and my mother and I would linger there by the domes of the old gas pumps under a bluish light. No chance to roll the windows down, not with all the bugs fanning out from the illuminated sign like a living haze, like rings around the moon portending rain. Ring at night, sailor take flight. And he wouldn't come back. An hour later he'd tap the window and make that circular movement of his thumb over the tops of his first two fingers: *give me money.* Give me your bills. She always had something in reserve, she never refused him, or me. He could always sense a game, some action, cards, or a slot machine. And from what I could tell, he always lost. He was a salesman, taking and being taken. The fundamental division of the universe: take or be taken, *film noir,* wise-guy cynicism. I make him into Bogart, but he was pure George Raft.

Some nights were so hot in our second floor apartment that we would drive thirty miles to the ocean, just to feel a breeze. I hope my father carried those memories as long as I have: what a culmination for a poor French-Canadian boy, driving to the ocean on a perfumed Florida night in the most expensive convertible on the road, past the planted rows of royal palms, their cement-gray, striated trunks like concrete pilings lining the road. It was a Hollywood dream of success, all flash and no substance, a salesman's skewered priority. Gatsby.

He could talk a state trooper out of a ticket, the sweet talk, the southernisms that just rolled off his tongue, "Why, officer, I didn't mean to go to do it!"

Mon erreur.

"Well, sir, you just see that you keep an eye on that speedometer from now on, all right?"

MOST NIGHTS HE WAS AWAY on the road. My mother and I would listen to the radio shows. When the dishes were done and the heat too oppressive, we'd walk those hibiscus-fragrant Florida streets, popping the camphor berries, slapping the mosquitoes, hoping to find a movie ("Air Cooled!") we could sit through. It didn't matter what. The sweet credulity of my generation.

I'm of the last generation for whom the movies trained my sentiments. All I knew of honor and manhood and beauty, of justice and evil, came from movies. On a lower note, all I knew of loyalty and villainy came from baseball, our struggling Leesburg Pirates and the nasty boys from Orlando. Who needed air-conditioning when you could watch Esther Williams slice the water? The last seduced generation for whom radio and the movies made the exotic—Los Angeles and New York—familiar and the familiar—love, sex, college, girls-next-door—exotic.

And the women! Not knowing what to do with them, I made each of them into imaginary sisters, adventures not with Dick and Jane but with Clark and Judy, Clark and Margaret O'Brien. I saw the fugitive charms of plain-but-virtuous-Janes long before the script revealed them. I knew to avoid the too-obviously glamorous long before my mother turned to me and whispered, "Don't ever fall for a girl like that!" The Hollywood stars with the golden hair, buxom girls in halter tops. Esther Williams, Betty

Grable, Jane Powell, and Ann Miller. Lips like the inside of hibiscus petals, without the ants. My mother couldn't take westerns, having ridden horses as a girl in western Canada. She'd embarrass me, holding her hands over her eyes, a grown woman like that. Nothing could be watched that killed Indians or glorified war.

SOMETIMES MY HAYFEVER was so bad we'd drive to the ocean with a wet towel around my head, and I'd lie there on a midnight beach as the waves flashed white and storm clouds rolled in, blotting out the stars. It was a revelation to me, like tadpoles and turtles eating the backyard fish—clouds at night!—cloud-patterns went on with no one to notice them. There was a kind of evil, thrilling, impersonal complexity to the world.

It's in the air these days, middle-aged children calling their parents back, Vivian Gornick and her mother, Philip Roth and his father, as the whiff of mortality reminds us we're far, far closer to death than childhood. We're afraid and repentent. We'd rather have them around in all their meddlesome, infuriating ways, than let them go. We'd be better sons now, we'd understand their panic just a little better. We'd understand because slowly, unavoidably, we're becoming them. We'd be *younger*, with our parents alive.

It's uncomfortable, even vaguely obscene, returning at fifty to the man who fathered me. ("They call us middle-aged," Alice Adams once wrote at sixty, "but how many hundred-and-twenty-year-olds do I know?") I'm two-thirds gone, with luck. We know now how they felt, staring down at us when we were teenagers. I was seventeen when he was my age now. He was a wrathful figure at fifty, and at his peak at fifty-two. I've written of him from a child's wonderstruck perspective, his power and potency, his furies and failings. Now I'm more *him* than me, or at least the me I was. Inevitably, not by choice, we become our parents. My father is the only man in my family who's been my age and survived it.

Good time, good money, salesman's lingo. I heard he's making good money over there. Look, son, three lanes up ahead, now we'll make good time!

"I'm Looking Over a Four Leaf Clover." The first post-war Fords, Art-Deco marvels, those '46 Fords, the pent-up designs. Everything is pent-up: desire, income, dreams. It is the first year I'm totally alive, singing all the songs on the car radio. The backseat child, taking it all in. "Peg O' My Heart." I know all those songs, because my father was a singer, and I learned them from him, not the radio. A childhood spent in the land of the giants.

—San Francisco, Iowa City,
Wellington, Buenos Aires
December 1991–April 1992

I began this book nearly three years ago and suspended it in despair. Then came an invitation from a geography professor at Laval University to contribute a paper for a conference on Québec—*la mère-patrie*—and Franco-America. Quebec City is a magic place for me, the city I'd fled to after my parents' divorce to learn my language and feel I belonged. Rare enough that Canada, let alone Québec, is the dark Pluto influencing several million Franco-American lives.

A Utah-born Québec geographer calling on me. How could I resist? He'd recognized our mirror-likeness: the preamble to the conference brochure was even taken from an old story of mine. In that novella, which was set in Manchester, the narrator, who resembles a possible-me (*si j'avais choisi le chemin de mon père*) remembers his father reminiscing over his years as a *journalier* in various parts of America. According to the father, in the '20s no town in America was farther than fifty miles from a French Mass. The shadow empire of New France and the *coureurs des bois* still lived in the river valleys of interior North America. Parishes in Kansas and Nebraska, Illinois and Ohio, still remembered the old ways and the old language.

(But I had made it up! Kansas French? I thought I was

being funny. My father never spoke to me of anything from his childhood, and the idea of a French Mass would have repelled him. But of course, as I was to learn at the Laval conference, it was true. Those parishes existed, those sons of the soil—strong, hard-working, hell-raising boys—entered America by skis, by snowshoes, with their fists, by a quick dash over the undefended border, with an address of relatives in Manchester or Lowell or Woonsocket, a mill-job waiting and no questions asked. With the inherited skills of carpentry and lumbering they could work their way to California if they wished, be driven from one town to the next, one church to the next and offered permanence through marriage, by the equivalents in their time of my old Saratoga woodcutter, J–P Comtois.)

The empowerment of the imagination. Did my story confirm the findings of the conference, or create them? If I have achieved sovereignty over my own experience, it is through imagination alone. I've been living this way for years, controlling a fantasy that bears sufficient likeness to reality to satisfy normal notions of sanity. Nothing that I can possibly imagine, so long as it relates to my parents, or to the southern world I knew as a child, no matter how improbable, violent, or surreal, is untrue. Under the shelter of their marriage, all things are possible. There really was a network of French parishes strung along the river systems of North America, still active in the early 1920s, *because I imagined them!* And so was William Kennedy with the Irish of Albany and Mordecai Richler with the Jews of Montréal. The whole world flowed through us. We were all a part of it, the great steaming ethnic saga of corruption, the cocaine-and-marijuana trade of its day.

Was my father a killer, shotgun loaded and trembling across his knees on those black Adirondack roads leading from Montréal to Troy, bringing in America's booze, paying off the small-town sheriffs for the rights of passage through their jurisdictions, shooting it out with would-be hijackers? You bet he was, *because I imagined it!* Ethnic lives contain dualities.

Yer dad's gatta rekkid lang's yam. . . .
Wanna meet an old-time Mafia Don? . . .
Barry Sisters, I hear Barry Sisters! . . .
Hey, Michael, where'd you get that tattoo? How come it's only a number? How come there's a line through the seven? That looks European or something. Yeah, I got it in Europe. A souvenir, so shuttup already, okay?

But when I try to discover my father's police record, his voice is laughing in my face. The private detective in Manchester, good French name, is a scam-artist, he takes the money, returns nothing. Tracking my father, I end up with the state's Attorney General, suing in small claims court.

Small claims would be a decent title for an autobiography.

So it was a Mormon voice speaking in French that announced the time for my journey home. Because of it, I went to Lac-Mégantic and looked up parish records. I began seeing my life pulled out of orbit by my father and seeing French-Canadian lives as a variant of Latin American.

RACISM IS THE TARNISHED THREAD that runs through the fabric of my life. I am a decently raised, liberal, blue-eyed white man; what better witness to the pervasiveness of race on this continent? I have researched it, I have been its witness and perpetrator in the segregated South, and finally, I am married to one of its victims. It enrages me that a medieval sickness should have determined so much of my life.

Lest an English-speaking Canadian read this and accuse me of blindness and favoritism, I'll admit I've been too apologetic for Québec. Garrison communities cannot help their pugnacious insularity. Québec governments of the last twenty years have been as dull-witted and spiteful as any segregationist or Afrikaner, or any Prince Edward Islander, in trying to stamp out ethnic diversity and thinking that purity can be preserved in the modern world (you can always try, but look at the company you keep). The Montréal police today harass Haitians as badly as they used to raid socialists, unionists, or Jehovah's Witnesses in my mother's time.

I spent most of the '80s looking for a permanent job—anywhere—but the demographics were wrong. We educated our sons on free-lancers' salaries, living first in Iowa so they could finish in a decent high school, then in New Jersey, British Columbia, Atlanta, Queens, and Manhattan where the part-time jobs led us. I'd been a tenured full professor at thirty-six; ten years later, I was virtually un-employable. Too white, too male, too old. For ten years I held a string of part-time jobs. The blemish that Bharati had felt in Canada, that she was the wrong race, that she must be somehow deformed to account for public reactions to her and to those like her, came to haunt me a decade later in the United States: this is what it is like to be too old, too experienced but too little known, too much pub-lished with too little to show for it. I could read the chair-men's minds as I went to interviews, made the short list: *your c.v. is very impressive. So how come I've never heard of you?* We used to joke in Canada: *if you're so good, how come you're still here?*

Bharati found work in New Jersey, taught five courses, finding a student to drive her home from her last class at midnight. I worked four part-time jobs in Man-hattan, a different campus each day, or night, of the week. We kept writing. My books got more and more Canadian, Bharati's more and more American. By the end of the decade, the times—the new consciousness of Asian im-migration, of multiculturalism—and Bharati's talents had come together. She went from not being able to afford milk and orange juice on the same table, to movie con-tracts, a distinguished professorship, Bill Moyers inter-views.

WE SAILED THROUGH OUR FORTIES without pensions or health-care insurance, renting in New Jersey, then in Long Island City, and finally subletting in Manhattan. My mother died and we used her savings—the untouched eighteen thousand of her divorce settlement—as a down payment on the cheapest pre-Crash co-op in the pioneering, Dominican-dominated east-into-Amsterdam fringe of the upper-Upper West Side. Three months later, the stock market crashed; so did gentrification. We were the last co-op building, adjoining and facing blank walls of rent-controlled tenements. Sixteen panhandlers staked the two blocks to the subway. Muggers hit us. The gentrifiers moved out and we were trapped.

Our super apologized for the rats—mice were our own lookout—because the street bridged an old underground river where they still bred. They came out of the sewers and up through the pipes. They took over the courtyard between our buildings. It became a fascination, watching them blanket the garbage sacks, an undulating gray wave. Watching in the winter, listening through our open, ground-floor windows in the summer. They picked their way over the wrought iron grating. The garbagemen attacked the mountain of green plastic sacks with baseball bats, whacking as they lifted, and the rats squealed their way across the sidewalk back to the safety of our building.

The joys of New York were all around us, but we had no time or energy or money to sample them. (I love New York.) Like hopeful New Yorkers, we took small pleasures, jogging down Riverside Drive, Symphony Space, a few dinners. In three years, we had no one to our place, we had no table. I started this book, but broke it off, too worried, too angry, too bitter to finish it.

When we came to New York in 1986, we thought our wanderings were over. We'd dreamed of New York, of making ourselves ready for New York. *We deserved New*

York. For twenty years we'd been monthly visitors from Montréal or Toronto or upstate. On nights when we went back to our hotel room or out to a friend's house in Jersey, we would look in the apartments—any apartment—and dream of what it must be like to wake up in Manhattan with your own furniture and your own *Times* at the door, your own cablevision, your own attitude.

The New York we came to was red-hot, the last flare-up before the cold collapse. We came too late, and the New York I capsulize is literary and cinemagraphic, other people's nostalgia. Even our oldest New York friends whose rent-controlled apartments were inherited from grandparents, or the artists who came to New York when it was the center of the world, or even those who came in the '70s and picked up monster apartments on pre-War scale for little more than our year's mortgage and maintenance, would leave if they could. They call me now. They ask, "What do you know about Kansas?"

A ND S O I S A I L E D the seas and came . . . to Iowa City.

In June 1990 I became the director of the International Writing Program at the University of Iowa. Unlike the Writers' Workshop, which teaches talented young Americans, the international program does not teach. It brings thirty-five established authors from every part of the world, many of whom speak very little English, for three months' residency in Iowa, exposing them to America, and vice-versa. (Outside of the United States, among writers the word *Iowa* is more likely to refer to the International Program than to the Workshop.) In its twenty-five years, eight hundred writers have attended, representing ninety countries. By now, many of those writers are among the best-known in the world, certainly the most respected in their own countries. Poetry is their passport.

(Thirty years ago, Bharati and I met as students and married in the Workshop. Paul Engle, the director at the time, introduced us on my first night in town. In 1967, Paul and his wife, Hua-ling, founded the International Program. Although I did not know him well, it would be difficult to name a man with greater practical influence over the course of my life than Paul Engle, who gave me: wife, profession, job, and now, hometown.)

A year later, I had a conversion experience.

In the summer of 1991, I was invited to Estonia and Finland as a USIA lecturer. In the final months of Soviet rule, Estonia had degenerated into mob-rule. Street gangs in Tallinn that controlled prostitution, drugs, vodka, and mugging rights to Finnish tourists had turned that seedy-elegant Hanseatic city into a scene out of *A Clockwork Orange*.

The poet who was my host served what food he could find—sour cream and rhubarb, dill and yoghurt, pork, and Moldavian wine in crystal glasses preserved from his wife's uncle's pre-War, pre-Russian jewelry store. We touched the rims of the glasses, chiming a toast with every sip. In that Baltic city, still light at midnight after the scenes of blood in the streets, it felt like a Thomas Mann story. "Disorder and Early Sorrow," perhaps: something grotesquely bourgeois. Protestant, Germanized communists seething under Russian and central Asian occupation. In Finland at the Lahti Writers' Conference a week later, I spoke on what I'd seen. The topic was "Memory, Europe, and the East-West Dialogue," a subject I'd been unable to address, even to imagine, before the trip to Estonia.

The contrast between the rattle of tire-irons crashing down the cobbled streets, boys bleeding in the center of intersections, and the tinkle of fine crystal in the poet's small apartment and the backdrop of Estonian choral music, seemed as strong, as insistent a symbol as anything in literature or out of my childhood. My job, which until then had been a high-level administrative and fund-raising post, became something new that summer. I don't know if a man should say of his job the same thing he might say of his wife or his country: *I began to fall in love with it.* After a decade of self-doubt, of wondering if streamers of toilet paper were stuck to my heel, or if I were exuding some sort of high-frequency odor that turned potential chairmen off, I had begun, again, to belong to something larger than myself. The world had begun again to speak in symbols. The world out there was linking up again with the permanent forms inside me.

I stayed on to visit Poland, the most densely-Iowized (over fifty) literary culture in the outer world. In Bydgoczsz, Gdańsk, and Warsaw I was greeted by writers and translators who'd been in the program. Nearly all of the Polish writers I, or the Engles before me, had hosted in Iowa, taken to parties, arranged readings and lectures for, had returned to Poland in the '70s and early-to-mid-'80s to certain imprisonment.

"What Solidarity was to the workers, Iowa was to the intellectuals," said one. Iowa kept their hope alive.

Now, many of the Iowa-returned writers are in the

new Polish diplomatic corps. They are the trusted ones, the people who kept culture and the language alive. From poet to ambassador. In a way, I felt the same way, fiction had been my passport as well—my books, all of which were dead and out of print, were a convertible currency.

DEAR READER: You know a few things about me, and one of them is that I have never performed useful social labor in my life. When I have earned, I have spent. When the money was scarce, we scrimped. I have saved nothing. Earnings from writing are untaxed at source; come tax-time, it all goes back. Like my father, if I were to die today there'd be nothing in the bank to pay the funeral expenses—that's the nature of the writing beast. I still believe there'll be some happy conjunction of movies and paperbacks and a late-life "discovery" that will save me from dependence on Social Security. And I also know, as Pascal once wrote, "because we are always planning to be happy, it is inevitable that we are never so."

How odd, then, that I should become, at this late stage in my life a convert to true-believerness, sending out the fund-raising letters, floating grants, proposals. How strange that I find myself writing in the 1991 "Program Report" that the revolutions we see around the world, particularly those in the former Soviet Union and Soviet Empire, are Iowa revolutions. That is, they are cultural and poetic far more than political and economic. It's the revolt of the Estonian wine glasses, the revolt of Saroyan relics, it's in the quote of the new Romanian ambassador to the United States in the *Times,* "Iowa changed my life."

And I too can say, Iowa changed my life.

That is the surface story.

I became invisible in the American '80s, a dead white male, with a reptilian pulse-rate. I began to feel that I didn't exist. I know now, in my fifties, that the struggle is not for fame or money or power, it is something much, much larger: to exist. To know I exist.

The danger is disappearance. Much of this book was written on a laptop computer while I was away from Iowa City. Nearly all of it was revised in various beds in various hotels and dark rooms, swatting the mosquitoes attracted to the screen, alone, or with Bharati sleeping next to me. New Zealand, Argentina, New York, Estonia, Finland, Poland, San Francisco, Germany, Holland, France, India, Canada—the travel of a year.

Under the surface of an active, check-writing life, there is mounting evidence to question my own existence. Not the obvious facts of drawing air and being paid, or like Camus' representative modern man, reading the papers and fornicating: it's something else. We deny the evidence of our senses if we do not have a concept broader than our senses to enclose them. If I don't have a concept of oceans, I won't see the waves. Canadians in the '60s and '70s, without a concept of Indian immigrants, couldn't see them. I remember trying to convince a bookstore at the foot of my street in Montréal to carry a copy of Bharati's first novel. They held the book (from Houghton-Mifflin), then looked at her picture. She looks Indian, they said. She is, said I. We don't carry foreign books, they said. She lives on this street, I answered. We don't carry foreign publishers, they said. You have other Houghton-Mifflin titles, I said. Look. Sorry, they said.

My ancient terror has never left me. It's the old question of identity, for whom and for what do I exist?

In *Making Sex,* the Berkeley historian Thomas Laqueur demonstrated that women did not exist until about 1800. There were females, of course, but only in the sense of being defective males. Female anatomy was an imperfect or distorted variant of the male. Lacking a concept of women, we couldn't see them. The classic anatomy texts failed to draw the most elementary distinctions. Sexual organs were drawn from unflattering angles, or distorted, to emphasize gender-equivalence. Lacking a concept of childhood, we saw children as defective adults. In *Ragtime,* E. L. Doctorow slyly points out that black people and immigrants did not yet exist, except as defective white people, or aspiring Americans who still had a long way to go. Political disputes in Argentina and El Salvador still rage over "the disappeared," a very different concept from the murdered. Canada has its so-called "visible" and "invisible" minorities, ("visible" or "invisible" to whom?) The dispute over the Columbus sesquicentennial is about continents, whole peoples, absenting themselves prior to 1492, so that they can be "discovered" by one coarse Italian.

I've learned from researching my father how fragile the records of birth and death can be, how suspect a parish entry, the impossibility of tracing any information even in my own family. My wife, like all non-Christian Indians of her generation, has no birth certificate. She exists only because she says she does. She has a birthdate and birthplace only because her parents established one. She has a *desh* because of ethnic memory.

Categories of people can suddenly *begin* to exist. "WASPs" didn't exist as a people—that is, as a tribal entity with predictable attributes—until a minority grew comfortable enough to counter-label them. White males, as a group, didn't exist until they became hegemonic chauvinist chromatist heterosexual militarist capitalists. I exist insofar as I oppress. Women and minorities exist in so far as they perceive a grievance; we are in danger of identifying ourselves through postures of victimization. A literary "canon" didn't exist as an oppressive and poisonous body of racist and sexist assumptions until the disempowered and decanonized grew confident enough to expose it as a negotiable construct. One reason the melting pot philosophy is beginning to fail in the United States is that the separate ingredients have begun calling the kettle white. It was constructed of an apparently nobler substance called Anglo-Saxon Protestantism that was exempt from tarnish.

In the years that we lived in Canada, Bharati did not exist because her concerns were perceived as not Canadian. After we moved to the United States, her work suddenly existed. It had relevance. (And mine disappeared. God is a symmetrist and our fates are perfect parabolas. Every point plotted on the upward curve is precisely repeated on the down side.) She became the vanguard voice for a new American consciousness, the new Americans from Asia in the American social fabric.

It is in all of those senses, then, I have begun to feel—and this is the anxiety with which I began this book—that my existence is imperiled. At the very moment that I travel the world representing American culture, I've yielded some sort of personal existence. I walk through walls, travel over borders, write the same paragraph in three different continents, conduct interviews in three languages on the same day. My existence is on the line. That is, it's *only* on the line, in the word, on this page.

And so this consciousness shuttles across the world, stitched together with a laptop computer. The laptop is a diver's oxygen tube. I write this line late at night in Iowa City. This afternoon, I taught Rushdie's *Shame* to a Writers' Workshop class. But yesterday morning in Buenos Aires I was being interviewed in French by an Argentine journalist, and after that I had lunch with the head of an Argentine foundation to explore funding possibilities for Argentine writers in Iowa City. This time last night I was buying souvenir T-shirts for my sons in the duty-free transit shops of Rio de Janeiro airport. At dawn, we pushed through Miami customs, at eight o'clock through O'Hare, at nine we arrived in Cedar Rapids, gateway to east-central Iowa, and at one o'clock, I taught Salman Rushdie.

Keneally, Rushdie, Naipaul, Atwood, Munro, Gallant, Mehta, Gordimer, Desai and a dozen others . . . I've written on each of them several times, taught their books every year, reviewed them in Canada or the States as their designated commentator. After a lifetime of teaching modern British, contemporary American, recent European, this is the group I've settled on. These are the writers I want to present to young Americans. They are the writers who are under my skin. Our lives seem interchangeable.

Writers from the edge of the universe are the authors

I know best, the ones I've quarreled with and made up with a dozen times. If I claim a clanship with them, it is over the sense of chaos, the unreality at the core of their lives. They too can doubt the sovereignty of their own experience, and colonialism is just a small part of it. It's the pace of change, the internalization of collapsing forms. I am their American outpost.

The literary world is vast, a grid with a million nodules, and the more I am in contact with it, the smaller I feel, a kind of worker-bee in the vast hive. The Whimsical Symmetrist is behind it all. Thirty years ago, when I was a student in the Writers' Workshop, coming out of a class in which I had read Musil or Céline, I felt I was a young colossus of literariness, preparing to take my place like Thomas Mann in a Borzoi edition. What I would finally choose to write about didn't really matter. I thought I had all human experience, all literature, all the great themes at my command. But the more I wrote, the smaller my compass became. I discovered I was tethered like a hound in a scruffy backyard.

THIS BOOK, which began by conjuring of my father from the memories of smoke, closes on my own vapor-trail. Concurrent with this book, a small Canadian publisher is bringing out a book of recent stories, *Man and His World,* which will be called, I'm certain, "autobiographical fictions." I can't escape the charge: what I most deeply imagine, or even invent, is assumed to be autobiographical.

Ray Carver, in one of his interviews once called my fiction "almost completely autobiographical," and while I appreciated the recognition, I had to take small exception. Everyone's fiction is almost completely autobiographical. What makes it fiction, usually, is its degree of disguise. So while most writers apportion or ascribe their own experiences to other characters, I somehow claim other people's experiences as my own. Once again, I am my father's son, only a more scrupulous liar. Until I see myself living their lives, in their houses, with their families as my own, other people don't exist. Until I see myself living in their countries, speaking their language, negotiating their streets on their buses, turning my key in their locks, I can't feel comfortable—I can't even feel that I've traveled. I have a hunger for accountability, for being everything my four grandparents and two parents made me, for capturing the headwaters of other people's memory-springs.

I am only what I can imagine myself to be; and I can imagine myself only in the parental matrix. My fiction is almost always about a self, roughly similar to myself, claiming its sovereignty under the dome of parental skies.

WHILE I WAS COMPLETING these last thoughts, riots broke out in Los Angeles in the wake of the jury acquittal of a police officer accused of assault on a black motorist. The assault had been videotaped, the whole world had seen it, and all of America had the basis of an informed opinion on it. The team of defense lawyers says "that videotape will be our defense." How can it be—we've all *seen* it! But, in true post-modernist fashion, the lawyers slowed down the tape, segmented it, commented upon it frame-by-frame, and that process was repeated day after day for several weeks before a suggestible jury, and a different reality emerged. A cartoon-reality, some might say, in which no one is hurt, no laws are violated, no motivation can be clearly detected. No pain, no shame. In fact, in the courtroom and jury-box, dream-logic, weightless dream-movement, replaced tedious old cause-and-effect. The suspension of consequence in a world of contingency: a lawyer's dream.

But history tells us: one man is beaten, and a city burns. The atom of injustice is split, and the energy destroys a community. There may not be accountability in the post-modern world, but there sure as hell is consequence.

I've tried to structure this book in the same way. Not to mislead and distort, but to isolate certain moments that have remained memorable, pivotal, poignant, and to forget about the flow. My life, viewed now from fifty-two years, is like a river that's been diverted for some upstream dam. Still some trickles in the deeper pools, and a lot of forgotten relics that sunk, and stayed.

Autobiography is always pulled in two directions: to seek coherence from chaos (how I rose above my humble origins, my early defeats, to lead this great country), or to question the meaning of any narrative (how my inherited faith in God, logic, and the ministrations of love all proved to be false and shallow). This book belongs more to the second school than the first, but with this important exception: there *is* a larger coherence. I'm not yet the person to claim it, and I don't have a theory or a faith to explain it, but I sense it at times in the patterns I've repeated, the coincidences that are no longer accidental, but part of an enormously complex fabric.

The riots of 1992 in Los Angeles got me to thinking of my own brief exposure to inner-city dynamics, in Cincinnati in 1951. I was in Samuel Ach Junior High for less than four months. In that time, I was robbed and assaulted, beaten by the authorities, robbed of my naïveté, childhood and innocence—and, I think, what touch of genius I possessed—taught fear and suspicion and given a new community to identify with, a community themselves of suspicious survivors. I was given a politics. That was over forty years ago, at a time of prosperity, simplicity (we like to think), radio dramas, Ozzie and Harrietness, yet it changed me forever.

Four months, such change! My lone experience as a racial minority.

There's another metaphor of post-modernism, or of The Persistence of My Father in All Things, that nudges into my consciousness now, although it happened in 1989 on my drive back to New York from Lac-Mégantic. I spent that night, before heading off in the morning to visit my Aunt Lena in her nursing home, with an old friend in Littleton, New Hampshire. I ran in the morning down his country road, saw a moose, felt myself in touch with a kind of vital spirit in the universe (if you know what I mean). As I was getting ready to leave, we walked around his property. A small hillock behind his house was a tangle of vines, flowers, and small fruit.

Pumpkins. Uncountable pumpkins! He had cut open a pumpkin the previous Hallowe'en, carved a face and stuck a candle in it, and when the holiday was over, thrown it off the porch into the light November snow. And in the spring, all the seeds had sprouted, and the pumpkin had replicated itself at least a hundred times.

Father!